SMART, SUCCESSFUL, AND BROKE

QUANTITY SALES

Most Dell books are available at special quantity discounts when purchased in bulk by corporations, organizations, and special-interest groups. Custom imprinting or excerpting can also be done to fit special needs. For details write: Dell Publishing, 666 Fifth Avenue, New York, NY 10103. Attn.: Special Sales Department.

INDIVIDUAL SALES

Are there any Dell books you want but cannot find in your local stores? If so, you can order them directly from us. You can get any Dell book in print. Simply include the book's title, author, and ISBN number if you have it, along with a check or money order (no cash can be accepted) for the full retail price plus $2.00 to cover shipping and handling. Mail to: Dell Readers Service, P.O. Box 5057, Des Plaines, IL 60017.

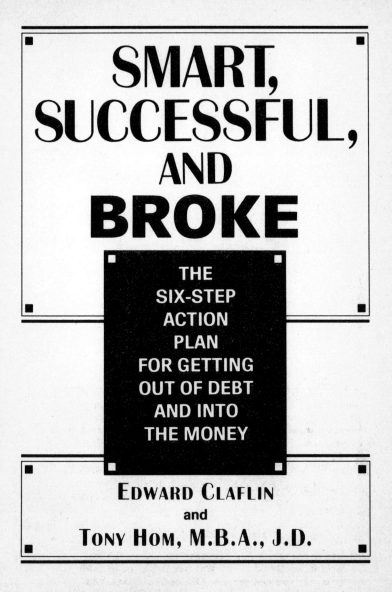

SMART, SUCCESSFUL, AND BROKE

THE SIX-STEP ACTION PLAN FOR GETTING OUT OF DEBT AND INTO THE MONEY

EDWARD CLAFLIN
and
TONY HOM, M.B.A., J.D.

A DELL TRADE PAPERBACK

A DELL TRADE PAPERBACK

Published by
Dell Publishing
a division of
Bantam Doubleday Dell Publishing Group, Inc.
666 Fifth Avenue
New York, New York 10103

ISBN: 0-440-50315-9

Design: Stanley S. Drate/Folio Graphics Co. Inc.

Printed in the United States of America

Published simultaneously in Canada

March 1991

10 9 8 7 6 5 4 3 2 1

BVG

Authors' Note

This publication is designed to provide accurate information in regard to the subject matter covered. This book is not intended as a substitute for legal, accounting, or other professional advice by a qualified professional. If legal advice or other expert assistance is required for any particular matter, the reader should seek the services of a competent professional person.

All character portrayals are composites based on actual case histories.

CONTENTS

Acknowledgments *xi*

You're Not the Only One in Debt *1*

1
THE SIX-STEP
ACTION PLAN

How to Use the Action Plan 17

STEP 1   Start a Financial Profile 28

STEP 2   Lock Up Your Credit Cards 37

STEP 3   Prepare the Lump-Sum, Tinker-Proof, Get-Through-the-Week, Don't-Fool-Yourself Budget Plan 46

STEP 4   Negotiate with Your Creditors 55

STEP 5   Get Back to the Future 67

STEP 6   Master Your Riches 77

Empowerment Through the Six Steps 87

2
SPECIAL TACTICS
FOR TOUGH TIMES

TACTIC 1 Dealing with Collection Agencies 93

TACTIC 2 Negotiating with the IRS . . . and
Other Tax Authorities 102

TACTIC 3 Negotiating with Utility Companies 105

TACTIC 4 Negotiating with a Landlord 111

TACTIC 5 What to Do If You Can't Meet Your
Mortgage Payments 114

TACTIC 6 Consolidating Your Debt 118

TACTIC 7 Checking Your Credit Report 122

TACTIC 8 Bankruptcy 129

3
RESOURCES

RESOURCE 1 Family and Friends 139

RESOURCE 2 Credit Counseling 143

RESOURCE 3 Attorneys 148

RESOURCE 4 Debtors Anonymous 151

4
APPENDIXES

Appendix A: Worksheets for Action Step 1   *155*

Appendix B: Worksheet for Action Step 3   *167*

Appendix C: Worksheet for Action Step 4   *173*

Appendix D: Demystifying the Jargon   *177*

Appendix E: Books on Investment and Financial
             Planning   *185*

■ ACKNOWLEDGMENTS

Both the authors would like to thank Henry Morrison, our agent, a master of tenacity, who not only helped to shape the book but also found it a happy home.

Jody Rein, executive editor at Dell, and Christine Benton, free-lance editor in Chicago, were hugely influential. Their querying, inserting, and rearranging helped to make this book far more accessible than it once was—all with the best interests of you, the reader, in mind.

We would also like to thank editorial assistant John Newsom and our publicist Bonnie Graves.

For the writer this has been a good collaboration—and I thank Tony Hom for being prepared to answer all questions at all times, no matter how naive they may have sounded. I also appreciate the help of Geoff Massey for his reading and comments on an early draft of the manuscript.

Behind the scenes was the best family a scribbler could hope for—my wife, Diana Mizer; my daughters, Jessica and Abigail; and, enduring in their optimism, my parents Dorothy and Beecher Claflin.

—EDWARD CLAFLIN

My thanks go to Ed Claflin; to my mother and father, May and Steve Chin; to my brothers, David Hom, James Hom, and Glen Chin; to my sister, Judy Tormey; and to my law partner, Sam Hwang.

—TONY HOM

SMART,
SUCCESSFUL,
AND
BROKE

You're Not the
Only One in Debt

Dave and Sarah are married professionals in their mid-thirties. Within the next two years Dave expects to make partner in a prestigious Philadelphia law firm, while Sarah, a former personnel director for an insurance company, is completing her M.B.A. in a six-year night-school program. Their oldest child, John, is in first grade; four-year-old Karen is in a private nursery school; and Susan, two, is in a part-time day-care program. They own two cars and have a four-bedroom house in the suburbs.

To all appearances a secure, happy, and prosperous family.

Yet Dave and Sarah felt desperate. Their debts were mounting. They were falling behind in all their monthly payments. And they were angry—so angry they could hardly talk to each other about the anxieties that were preying on them.

And their situation was getting worse every month. Their credit card accounts were borrowed up to the limit. Their last three mortgage payments had been late. They'd drained their savings. And they'd drawn their full line of credit at the bank.

Recently they had been considering drastic measures.

They could sell one of their cars. But how would they get along without it?

Sarah could drop her night-school courses. But if she sacrificed her M.B.A., she would just be throwing away future earning power.

Of course they could stop eating out. But they counted on a few nights out as a respite from their hectic pace.

They could skip vacation this year. But would they really *save* that vacation money—or just spend it somewhere else?

Where *was* their money going?

Each blamed the other. Sarah listed some questionable investments that Dave had made. Dave saw Sarah as indulging the children—spending too much on new toys and clothes and not saving anything for the family's "education fund."

But when Dave and Sarah looked at their situation more closely, they realized that neither of them had a clear idea *where* their money was going. Both of them readily admitted they were in a mess.

But neither of them knew *why*.

■ ■ ■

Nancy is a magazine editor—a single, divorced woman with one child in a two-bedroom rented apartment. She is $20,000 in debt on credit card charges. She takes freelance work to supplement her income and help pay for day care—but even so, she is paying only the minimum on her charge cards each month. At this rate it will take her up to 10 years to pay them off—*if* she doesn't add any more charges, *if* her salary rises, and *if* no unforeseen emergencies arise.

■ ■ ■

George is a 26-year-old graduate of law school. He is married with one child. His wife, who is at home with the baby, does not have an income.

George is $40,000 in debt with student loans—and without a job offer that looks attractive. He's given himself one more month to look, and he's decided that after that he'll take the first offer that comes along, no matter what it is.

■ ■ ■

Patty is a 34-year-old management consultant who travels at least four out of every five working days and is often out of town on weekends. Five years ago she decided that real estate was her best long-term investment, and she bought a small house in an upscale neighborhood. To pay her bills she has authorized automatic payments from checking on her mortgage, gas, electricity, insurance, and other monthly expenses. Her salary is direct-deposited by her employer into the same checking account.

Patty has three credit cards that she uses constantly and interchangeably for both business and personal expenses. Although she submits business receipts and a monthly expense report to her employer, she sometimes uses the reimbursement check to pay for personal expenses rather than sending it directly to her credit card account.

The outstanding balances on all three cards now average $1,500, and she's paying only the minimum charges each month. Her end-of-the-year bonus—which turned out to be half what she expected—was spent before it arrived. She just got a letter from the bank saying her account is overdrawn, and she doesn't know why.

■ ■ ■

Terry, a business school graduate, is director of market research for an advertising firm. He pays mortgage and maintenance on a one-bedroom co-op apartment in a doorman building in the city. Terry belongs to a health club, and he's a sports fan who gets to hockey and basketball games whenever he can. He has an active social life.

Last year Terry got rid of the Nissan he'd been driving for five years and bought a Saab 900 Turbo that he parks in his building. He has eight credit cards, charge accounts at five department stores, and an oil company card. On three of his credit card accounts he's more than 60 days overdue. On four of them he's borrowed up to the limit. In addition, he's paying off a school loan.

Terry hasn't been able to save anything. He's living from paycheck to paycheck. He's determined to pay off two of his cards when his next bonus comes through. And he's counting on a big raise next year.

If You're in Debt, You Have Plenty of Company!

If you saw yourself when you read about the financial situation of Dave and Sarah, George, Nancy, Patty, or Terry, you are certainly not alone.

Millions of Americans today have similar stories.

Of course indebtedness is nothing new to the American way of life. What is new in the 1990s is the special combination punch of exploding costs and slowly increasing real earnings. This one-two punch has left most of us with minuscule savings—and more debt than our parents and grandparents could have imagined in their wildest nightmares.

It's not our fault that many of us are in tough economic situations. The pinch that we're experiencing is being felt by many. From the mid-sixties to the mid-seventies the average American family with two children doubled its

income (in inflation-adjusted dollars), from $14,000 to
$28,000. From the mid-seventies to the mid-eighties the
same "average family" experienced a *decline* of about
$1,600 in real earnings. While income recovered slightly in
the late eighties, many baby boomers feel they are less well
off than their parents were at their age.

Few individuals or families can save very much. As a
percentage of disposable personal income, personal savings
were above 9 percent in 1973; in 1987 savings bottomed
out at around 3 percent of take-home pay. As more families
with children have started to save for future college costs,
savings have gradually risen. But by 1990 the majority of
us were still saving only about 6 percent of our after-tax
income.

Meanwhile credit card purchases have shot up from
$53 billion in 1979 to $214 billion in 1989—400 percent in
just ten years. With 795 million credit cards in circulation
in the U.S., the average consumer now carries six or seven,
including three retail cards, two bank cards, and one oil
card. In early 1990 the average credit card debt stood at
$1,100 per household.

Credit has been easy to obtain, and in the 1990s
lenders are more eager than ever to take advantage of our
urgent need to shop and spend. Banks and credit card
companies are urging their customers to borrow more.
Department stores plead with us to use their cards and buy
their goods. Lending institutions want us to take cash
advances.

Most of us are all too familiar with the lure of credit
cards. Preapproved lines of credit range from $2,000 to
$10,000, with interest rates ranging from 15 percent to 24
percent per year. Cash advances account for more than 12
percent of all charges on credit cards. Financial observers
agree that the American consumer is more extended now
than at any time since World War II. Many of us are using
credit to pay for luxuries, entertainment, and sometimes
necessities too. As we all know, the costs of food, housing,

health care, education, and other essentials are rising steadily, and most salaries aren't keeping pace.

Fear and Self-Loathing in Credit Land

When there's been an upward spiral of spending without a corresponding increase in income, the monthly ordeal of paying bills begins to resemble an evening in purgatory.

When debts seem overwhelming, we get scared.

Maybe you can't pay the rent on your apartment. Or maybe you're having trouble making a mortgage payment on your home. Or collection agents are trying to reach you. Or credit card companies are threatening to turn your account over to a collection agency. You might be struggling to get your family through the month—or you're having trouble looking ahead to what's going to happen next year. Whatever the problem, the emotional reaction to debt is generally the same.

Panic.

We probably don't need to remind you that there's no such thing as debtor's prison, the poorhouse, or being drawn and quartered for late payments on credit card accounts. But that knowledge doesn't alleviate much anxiety, does it? That's because what's really scary is the loss of control that heavy indebtedness represents to most of us. We don't know how we got into this mess or how to get out of it. So we panic.

Unfortunately, we may also keep those fears strictly to ourselves. And how can anyone help you if no one knows you're in trouble?

Debt is not something we usually discuss casually with friends or relatives. In fact many of us hide our fears about running out of money from those who are closest to us. We don't want our own families to be concerned—and most of us are reluctant to confess our financial troubles even to our best friends.

When we can't pay our debts, we may feel as if it's "all catching up with us." When personal finances are out of control, we often feel as if our entire *lives* are out of control. We feel guilty. We feel as if it's all our fault.

Isn't indebtedness a sign that you can't quite handle things? Doesn't it mean that you're financially irresponsible?

Not necessarily.

Just by picking up this book you've shown that you are ready to take control of your debt—and your life.

This book can help you do just that. In the following pages we'll provide you with some solutions to the dilemma that you may be facing today, addressing the *panic* of indebtedness as well as the *problem*. We'll introduce you to a specific, straightforward *action plan,* a step-by-step approach to getting your household budget in order, dealing with creditors, and looking ahead to the future.

But first, an objective look at debt and credit should begin to alleviate some of your fears.

A Household in Debt

Debt problems were affecting every aspect of Dave and Sarah Lambert's lives—their careers, their relationship, their children. They were two educated, successful young people who were watching everything get out of hand when it should have all been in good order.

What had they done wrong?

They were in debt, certainly.

But they hadn't done *anything* wrong.

The first thing they needed to get over was the fear that they had made a mistake somewhere.

Yes, Dave and Sarah may have overspent here and there.

Yes, they were living somewhat beyond their means.

Yes, they could have planned more carefully.

Possibly, they had made some unwise investments.

Nonetheless, they were on the right track. They had a lot of good things going for them. They were responsible, hardworking individuals who wanted the best for their children. They valued professional achievement and were willing to make personal sacrifices for long-term personal enrichment and financial rewards. They respected their obligations and honored their financial commitments (hence their excellent credit rating, which had allowed them to continue borrowing!). And they understood the value of making investments for the future.

THE VALUE OF CREDIT

A first step for Dave and Sarah was to recognize the value of the credit they had established over the years.

In the grip of their immediate dilemma they had begun to lose sight of the financial power they had obtained by incurring and paying off debt. They had provided themselves with professional growth, a beneficial community environment, excellent educational opportunities for Sarah and the children, enriching activities for the family, and the freedom to make many kinds of personal choices.

But in their desperation they had begun to fantasize about a world in which they were completely debt-free. No credit card payments. No car loans. No school loans. No home-improvement loans. No debt obligations of any kind!

Pure fantasy, of course. And it was a little dangerous for them to think that way.

If they tried to work toward this completely unrealistic goal—if they tried to get out from under *all* their obligations—they wouldn't be able to do it. And, being achievers by nature, when they didn't reach their impossible goals, they would become discouraged and fall back into their old spending patterns.

What their panic kept them from seeing was that it was *over*-indebtedness—not indebtedness itself—that was creating problems for them.

Dave and Sarah would never be absolutely debt-free. This wasn't even a desirable goal. They simply needed to organize their debt so it would continue to serve them as beneficially as it had in the past.

Keys to Controlling Debt

Management is always the key. But good management requires sound goals and rational planning. What Dave and Sarah needed was to get control over their spending habits so they could gain control over their lives again. Once they controlled their debt, it would stop controlling them.

In a few meetings with an attorney—but above all by attacking the situation together—Dave and Sarah worked out a plan of action.

Within a week they had taken the first step in the six-step action plan for dealing with their creditors, getting on their feet again, and working toward future goals.

Within a month they were operating on a new budget.

Within three months they were comfortably managing their debt obligations and beginning to set aside small amounts of money in special accounts. Within two years they had paid off a number of their creditors and were able to reallocate some of their payments toward investment funds.

WHAT IS THE MAGIC FORMULA?

There isn't any.

Dave and Sarah simply had to get control of their budget. They had to discover the debt-creating activities that were seriously draining their financial resources. Once they put a halt to the spending that created debt, their debts diminished automatically.

The fact is, almost no situation is hopeless. If you are fully employed, earning a steady income, and serious about improving your financial position, *debt is never an unmanageable problem*.

Of course the situation is much more serious if you are unemployed, burdened with extraordinary medical expenses, or overtaken by financial reverses. But even in these cases of extreme duress the most important thing is not to panic. There are resources you can utilize, people you can turn to, and unexplored routes you can take to relieve yourself of the emotional stresses that go along with financial hardship.

Millions of Americans are in circumstances similar to Dave and Sarah's. But most debt problems can be solved without going into bankruptcy. Initially, getting free and clear involves concentration and hard work. But once the old patterns have been broken and new ones established in their place, staying free and clear is no more work than staying in debt.

Fortunately, personal financial planning often has very little to do with percentage points and detailed allocations. You don't have to be an expert money manager to create a workable home budget. Managing your money usually depends on a variety of factors *apart from* smart accounting.

Here are some of the tasks and tools involved in the work of getting free and clear:

CHANGING PATTERNS, BREAKING HABITS

Surprising as it may seem, managing debt can often be done with very little sacrifice. It is not spending, per se, that puts individuals or families into debt but *uncontrolled spending* that can lead to near-disaster. Quite often uncontrolled spending is a habit.

Changing patterns won't happen overnight. But you have to work on your patterns of spending if you want to eliminate the "minus" behavior that's eroding your "plus" behavior. Once you recognize the patterns that lead to overspending, you can change those patterns to fit your actual budget. Step 1 of our action plan gives you all the data you need to identify patterns in your spending behavior.

A MARGIN OF COMFORT

For some people excessive spending is merely a way to say "I'm a risk taker." In other words it's a positive affirmation of personal independence.

But risk taking doesn't *have* to take place in the dangerous territory of the household budget. There are ways to affirm that kind of freedom without turning your personal life into a nightmare or threatening the security of those who depend on you.

Managing debt means having a margin of comfort. With that margin you can enjoy what you can really afford instead of trying to afford what you impulsively spend. You can take greater risks in other areas because you have a greater sense of command over your own destiny.

Managing debt isn't easy. If you truly want to solve the financial problems you're facing, there must be times when you say no to yourself and to others in your household.

But when *no* has a purpose, it's not a sacrifice. When it leads to greater returns in terms of family happiness, financial prosperity, and personal enjoyment, *no* can be the most rewarding word in your vocabulary. Saying no to credit cards in step 2 of our action plan, for example, is an affirmation that you can have a very satisfying life-style—and still feel good about yourself—even if you can't spend money on everything in the world you want.

AFFIRMING PRIORITIES, RECOGNIZING EXPECTATIONS

After you've identified spending patterns, you have to be honest with yourself so you know why you're spending and what those expenditures mean to you personally. Only then can you successfully change those patterns. For example, if you're an avid reader and you unrealistically vow to cancel all your periodical subscriptions, you're dooming yourself to failure.

Affirming priorities is a key to controlling debt. You can't have it all. You can't *do* it all. But money management is not an all-or-nothing game. You need to decide what's first on your list, what's last, and what items can be negotiated in the middle.

And in doing so, and planning for your future, you must recognize your personal expectations. You have to think about where you are now and where you expect to be in a few years. Are your professional and income goals realistic?

And what about other people's expectations? Are you trying to live up to someone else's image of you—and paying an emotional price (as well as an economic price) for doing so? The financial profile that easily emerges from step 1 of our action plan can serve as an effective evaluative tool for the rest of your life.

COMMUNICATING, NEGOTIATING

If you're married, are you facing your money problems together?

Families differ in the way they handle the household finances, but most systems are based simply on tradition and habit. In a family where one parent is working, that person might be the keeper of the budget as well as the provider. Or one spouse brings home the paycheck, but the other pays most of the bills.

In the two-paycheck, two-checkbook household, husband and wife may have separate domains of income and expenses. Often the pattern is established early in the marriage and then just maintained with occasional variations.

When the household is prosperous and all the bills are paid, we naturally assume that the "system" (whatever it is) works well. Why change it? But in a stressful debt situation one person may begin to blame the other. It's an easy pattern to fall into. Who's not earning enough? Who's spending too much? Whose idea was it to take that expensive vacation, throw that lavish party, or get all the options on a new car? Once the "blaming" pattern begins, money issues become inflammatory. So many couples say "We can't talk about it. We end up fighting."

How can we break this pattern?

The key to communicating effectively about finances is to concentrate on the *system*. How does it work? Who's responsible for what? How do spouses—or living-together partners—make decisions about shared income and expenses? Once these issues are raised and discussed, they won't be miraculously solved. It takes commitment and patience on everyone's part. But the great reward is that partners can begin to *feel* like partners working together to solve the problem, rather than facing it alone. And if you have children, they need to be considered and involved as well. The whole family must be working toward the same goal if *any* goals are to be reached. We'll discuss the importance of this issue throughout the six steps.

And let's not forget others with whom you must communicate: creditors, parents, and friends might be in a position to help. Better communication and negotiation can speed you on your way to being free and clear.

Skills for Managing Debt

Again, none of these slight shifts in behavior requires you to master the skills of an accountant. In fact, once you have established new patterns for managing your debt, you may spend much less time on monthly bills and budgeting than before.

Establishing those new patterns is the key. And to do that you need help—the kind of help that we'll be giving you in this book.

There are no secrets to instant success in personal

money management. But if you have the ability to negotiate with people and balance a checkbook, there's nothing to prevent you from taking full control over the management of your domestic finances. And you'll discover for yourself how credit can become a tool to use in many different ways, rather than a threat to your financial security.

If you make full use of the resources mentioned in this book, seriously follow the guidelines for dealing with your situation, and pursue the action steps that we propose, you are already well on the road to controlling your debt so it doesn't control you.

You're smart. You're successful. And there's no reason why anxiety about debt should make you feel less smart or less successful than you really are. That's why we recommend *action*.

I

THE SIX-STEP ACTION PLAN

How to Use the Action Plan

You're ready to take action. Whether the alarm that's ringing in your head manifests itself as a vague, nagging feeling of financial discomfort or an eruption of full-blown panic, you know it's time to do something.

But wait. In all the other areas of your life you've been successful. And you didn't achieve that by launching head-first into the unknown. Whenever you've had a problem to solve or a goal to reach, you've approached the task with a plan. So in this introduction we're going to tell you exactly how to proceed with the six-step action plan—how to recognize the action signals, what you'll be doing in each step, and when to do it.

17

Take Your Cue: Recognizing the Action Signals

Before you read about the fundamentals of the six action steps, put your financial status into concrete terms: translate those *feelings* about your situation into *facts*.

On the following pages are "The Signals" and "Action Clues" that tell you where you stand and how you should use the rest of this book.

How do you know if you are carrying too much debt?

That's not necessarily an easy question to answer. Usually the signals are just a gradual accumulation of annoyances that turn into frustrations and finally into major anxieties.

There are some objective, quantitative signs that your debts may be too high. But just as significantly, there may be some behavior patterns that indicate your spending is out of control.

You should be able to identify your particular cues to take action in a matter of minutes—no fancy accounting gimmicks required. (If, however, you need a brief review of a few basic terms, you'll find a "refresher course" in Appendix D, pages 177–183.)

WHAT, YOU WORRY?

Whether your debt is secured or unsecured, you *don't* need to worry about it as long as the following facts are true for you.

THE SIGNALS

1. You are meeting all your payments and not exceeding your credit limits; *and*
2. You're paying all your monthly bills; *and*
3. You have at least two months' salary set aside (or invested) in case you have an emergency; *and*

4. You are currently following a budget plan that will help you meet your future goals.

If this is your situation, you're all set, even if you feel like you have a lot of debt. Since you're meeting your payments on time, you're actually creating a great-looking credit record. Since you can pay all your monthly bills, you obviously have no financial hardship. With two months' salary set aside, you have the security of knowing that you could take care of yourself (and your family) for a while in case of emergency. And if you have a financial plan that's working, you will be able to meet your future goals, whether those goals are more entertainment and leisure, new property and investments, further education for yourself, or (if you have a family) education and some security for your children's future.

If you picked up this book, however, it's quite likely that the above "signals" do not fully describe your current financial situation. Perhaps they describe the position you'd *like* to be in—but you're not quite there yet. If that's the case, many parts of this book can help you get your financial house fully in order, especially the financial profile in step 1.

And you might not need to go past step 1 unless a future need arises. If that occurs, review the next set of signals.

DOES OVERINDEBTEDNESS SOUND LIKE YOU?

Let's look at the signals that tell you that your liquidity is in jeopardy and/or you have fallen into a pattern of overspending. Have you received the following signals?

THE SIGNALS

Too Little Cash . . .

1. Your monthly payments on unsecured debt are too high in comparison to your income. Without wor-

rying about precise figures, take a rough tally of your monthly take-home pay and that of any other household members. Then quickly add up your monthly minimum credit card payments. Divide your payments by your pay. If you get a figure greater than .20 (20 percent), you're overextended. At some point your ability to meet current household expenses is likely to be jeopardized.

2. You are not able to pay the minimum monthly charges on your credit card accounts—but you still use those credit cards. Eventually you'll probably have to default on some payments.

3. You're applying for *new* credit cards just to keep current with your payments on *old* ones. You're going to run out of money in your future.

4. You consistently wait for the second or third notice from credit card or charge card companies. No one needs to tell you that you have too many outstanding debts. Unless this is due to a temporary personal, household, or employment situation, those notices are a signal that you need to do something about your household budget.

5. You are drawing increasing amounts from a line of credit at the bank—with no prospect of paying it back. You're undoubtedly thinking "What will happen when I've used up all the line?" Your answer may be "Open a new line," but you can foresee a day when eventually you won't be able to make all those payments.

. . . Too Much Spending

1. You fill out and send in new credit card applications that come to you in the mail because you need that credit to pay for your daily bread. Of course it's fine to apply for a new credit card if you're just beginning to establish creditworthiness or if your income has risen and you can afford the time payments on

new debt. But if you find yourself thinking "Thank God—just in time!" when a new application comes through the mail, consider yourself overindebted.

2. You make vacation plans without having any idea how you'll pay for the vacation. Using credit cards on vacations is a way of life, of course. But when those charges come through, they create a major lump deficit in the account. If last year's vacation isn't paid for by the time you take your vacation this year, you're in a deficit spending pattern that's building rather than decreasing.

3. You have already *over*spent an anticipated salary raise, bonus, or tax refund before you bring it home. Of course, if you spend exactly the right amount, you're fine. But a remarkable number of us tend to overspend in the expectation of windfall profits that don't arrive in the amounts that we had anticipated.

4. You use money as a mood elevator, spending it "when you're down" on such things as:

- Clothing
- Impulse buys (By definition: you don't know you need something or that you're going to buy it until you happen to walk into a store and see it!)
- Catalog shopping
- Gift buying

ACTION CUES

Take action steps 1–6 as soon as possible. If you've received the signals of too little cash or too much spending, the sooner you discover the depth and source of the problem, the sooner you can solve it.

• Quickly read the chapters on all six steps so you'll know what your tasks are going to entail.

• Refer to one or more of the special tactics in Part II if your review of the six steps signals you need more help in a particular area:

Dealing with Collection Agencies
Negotiating with the IRS . . . and Other Tax Authorities
Negotiating with Utility Companies
Negotiating with a Landlord
What to Do If You Can't Meet Your Mortgage Payments
Consolidating Your Debt
Checking Your Credit Report
Bankruptcy

• Become aware of your resources. Part III of this book will guide you to some private and public resources that are available when you set out to resolve a debt problem. There are numerous avenues for seeking help, from your own relatives and friends to the professional services of lawyers and credit-counseling agencies. But it's important to know what you're looking for, what questions to ask, and—in the case of professional services—what to expect from the people who advise you. Refer to this section whenever you feel you don't know where to turn for help.

ARE YOU IN SERIOUS DEBT?

Even when collection agencies are calling or legal notices are arriving in the mail, we may wish to deny that the situation is anything more than "temporary." And it may be. But even if it *is* a temporary situation, it needs our immediate attention if creditors are threatening to take action that could jeopardize our homes, our security, or our ability to earn a living.

THE SIGNALS

Without question, the situation demands attention if the following signals are coming your way.

1. Your landlord is threatening eviction, or your mortgage holder has sent you a foreclosure notice.

2. Creditors or collection agents are threatening you with legal action that could lead to levies or liens on your property or to garnishment of wages (the taking of part of your salary directly from your employer to satisfy a creditor).
3. You have received notices about legal action from the IRS or from state or city tax collectors.

ACTION CUES

Take action now.

You can't afford to delay, and you'll have to take all six steps posthaste, but your particular situation may dictate a different sequence:

If your creditors are sending collection notices or calling you right now, go directly to step 4: negotiate with your creditors. This is a situation that will only get worse if you postpone talking to your creditors. It's still important to take all the other steps of the action plan. (In fact it's extremely urgent that you do so. But in the meantime you'll need to negotiate with your creditors using some of the methods described in step 4 or using some of the special tactics in Part II.)

If you are threatened with legal action, eviction, or foreclosure, refer right now to Parts II and III. You'll need special tactics and resources to take care of your immediate difficulties so you have some room to take step-by-step action.

If you are an uncontrolled user of credit cards, take step 2 before step 1. Before you do anything else, begin the action plan by locking up your cards.

There's a simple "uncontrolled user" test. If you identify one or more signals that you are in serious debt (using the criteria listed above) and you *still* use plastic to make nonessential purchases, then your use of credit cards is definitely out of control.

The Six Action Steps

If you are so concerned about money that you can't get your financial problems out of your mind, it's time to make a deal with yourself.

This deal isn't going to spell the end to all your joys, your pleasures, or your satisfactions in life. What it *can* do is to help put an end to your anxiety, give you a sense of confidence, and allow you greater control over your finances.

Here's the deal:

STEP 1: START A FINANCIAL PROFILE

This is a matter of keeping track of daily expenses, then adding them up to get a monthly profile. By the end of this month you'll have a pretty good idea of *what* you are spending and *where*. (If your expenses are very consistent from week to week, you may be able to complete step 1 in less than a month, but we recommend a full month for reliable accuracy.)

As you prepare this profile, you may have some moments when your hands sweat and your temples pound—this is, after all, your *secret* financial life. But it's absolutely necessary to get through this step so you can figure out what to do next.

STEP 2: LOCK UP YOUR CREDIT CARDS

Yes, just the thought of that step may cause a chill of panic. But if you do it, you're going to be getting a whole new dimension of security. It's not as hard as you might think to give up plastic. You could be saving yourself thousands of dollars—and probably a lot of insomnia—when you take this step. It takes exactly 60 seconds to lock up your cards after you've completed step 1.

STEP 3: PREPARE THE LUMP-SUM, TINKER-PROOF, GET-THROUGH-THE-WEEK, DON'T-FOOL-YOURSELF BUDGET PLAN

This is the best way we know to get rid of the many intricacies of home-budget planning—and simplify both your accounting and your financing. The cash-only plan will help to keep you within a weekly spending limit while you get your other accounts in order. We'll show you how to budget for the lump-sum method, and we'll demonstrate why it works so well. By referring to your financial profile, you can prepare this budget plan in an evening. You will start using the budget plan as soon as it's prepared.

STEP 4: CALL YOUR CREDITORS

In many cases you can work out a payment plan with your creditors that will be fair and equitable and within your budget. As soon as you've finished preparing your budget plan, you should begin making the necessary calls and writing follow-up letters to negotiate with your creditors.

STEP 5: GET BACK TO THE FUTURE

Here's the payoff for the deal that you're making with yourself. As you get greater control over your financial life, you're going to plan those pleasures that make life worthwhile—but in the future you don't have to dread the financial aftermath. By the time your creditor payments are settled, you will know how much you're going to have left over from the lump-sum budget you've been using. You can begin to set up the accounts that help you plan your pleasures and prepare for future needs and necessities.

STEP 6: MASTER YOUR RICHES

The total objective is not just to get you out of debt but also to help you plan for a more prosperous future. To master your riches you need to make the most of your own skills, your resources, and your ability to handle money. You also need to set financial goals.

From your current financial position, getting to the point where you master your riches may seem a long way off. But the way could be clearer and the distance shorter than you think—if you make a deal with yourself to follow all six steps of this plan.

■ **GET YOUR FAMILY ON THE PLAN**

If you are married, you and your spouse should both read this book and agree that you both will follow the six-step action plan. Discuss it.

If you have children, you need to include them in your discussion.

What you tell the children depends on their ages, of course. But no matter how old they are, it's important for them to know about changes that are likely to affect their life-style, their allowances, or their spending.

A young child might be frightened if he or she just hears that you "can't afford" things that you need to purchase automatically. ("Are we getting poor?" one five-year-old asked her mother.) Young children need reassurance that you have a plan and that their needs will be provided for.

The action plan will definitely affect older children who are already spending money on their own. They need to know what their options are. If their allowances are going to be reduced, can they start earning and saving for themselves? Are there ways they can help the whole household?

If you have a full or partial support of parents or in-laws, it's essential for you and your partner to discuss the action plan with them. Although they may be largely dependent on you, they might also be able to suggest other sources of income or suggest ways that they can help out.

When you, your spouse, and everyone else in the household is working together on the action plan, your whole family becomes a resource. Yes, there are likely to be moments of doubt and tension. But those moments will come less often if you all approach the plan together from the very beginning.

Putting It on "Automatic"

Once you've taken these six steps, the system is self-perpetuating. Admittedly the hardest work is up front, where all the hardest work should be. But once you mobilize the plan, it works by itself. Budgeting becomes easier. Paying bills becomes easier. And it's certainly a lot less time-consuming to establish a pattern and follow it than to be constantly negotiating with your own conscience and with others in your household about each dollar you spend.

Coming Up . . . Action!

The action steps in Part I require one important thing from you: commitment. If you identify your debit activities and do nothing about them, in all likelihood your debt problems will just get worse. But if you begin to take action immediately by implementing the six-step action plan, you can begin to realize what it means to have control over your personal security and financial future. And that's a great feeling!

START A FINANCIAL PROFILE

Someone once likened this process to an out-of-body experience. An out-of-checkbook experience would be more like it. Essentially what you're going to do is stand back from your financial situation—emptying your mind of angst, doubt, and suffering—and take a look at where you actually spend your money. You are going to keep track of all your daily, weekly, and monthly expenses. You're going to list your credit card and charge card payments. You're going to add up your monthly take-home pay. And you're going to use all that information to set some spending goals for the next month.

Setting Out

Appendix A contains three worksheets for you to use in preparing your financial profile—an Expense Worksheet, a Credit Card and Charge Card Worksheet, and an Income Worksheet.

In step 1 you will be collecting all the data you need—preferably over one month—to fill out these worksheets, which will tell you exactly where the money that's coming in and the money you're borrowing are going.

As you set out, you'll follow this simple schedule:

EVERY DAY

1. Keep all receipts in your wallet or an envelope. At the end of each day, put all these receipts in a single shoe box or envelope that's clearly marked "Daily Expenses."

2. Use a small "Expenses" notebook to make entries that aren't covered by receipts. Make a notation alongside each entry so you know what you spent the money on. At the end of each day, turn over a new page.

It is essential to be honest with yourself and list *everything* that you spend. If you buy a lunch that cost "just a few dollars," keep a receipt or write down how much it cost. If you pick up "a few items" at the drugstore on your way home, note what those items were and how much you actually spent on them. If you go to a movie and have a popcorn and soda, keep track of the cost of the movie, the cost of the popcorn, and the cost of the soda.

All this may seem very picayune. And in fact you may wonder whether you're supposed to be turning into Super-Accountant.

You're not.

But you *are* going to find out where you really spend your money—thinkingly, unthinkingly, or on autopilot.

EVERY WEEK

At the end of each week you will need some time to enter all the expenditures for the week. (This will probably take less than an hour.)

The Expense Worksheet in Appendix A is set up like this:

EXPENSE WORKSHEET

EXPENSE	WEEK 1	WEEK 2	WEEK 3	WEEK 4	TOTAL	GOAL
_____	☐	☐	☐	☐	☐	$ ____

In the left-hand column of the worksheet are listed most of the usual household expenses. If some of these expense items don't apply to you or your household, just skip over them. On the other hand, if you have additional expenses not included in this list, enter them in the spaces provided.

Be sure to include *every* item in your household budget. Since the purpose of filling out this profile is to tell you exactly where you spend your money during the course of a month, it's important to be as detailed as possible.

1. Add up the amounts in each category, referring to your receipts and notebook. Ask all household members who spend money to bring their receipts and notebooks.

2. Enter the total on the line for each expense item.

AT THE END OF THE MONTH

Total Your Expenses

1. Enter your once-a-month expenses—rent or mortgage, car payments, utility bills, etc.—in the appropriate columns on the Expense Worksheet.

2. Calculate expenses that are paid quarterly, annually, or semiannually on a *monthly* basis. For instance, if a home insurance premium is paid annually, divide the premium by 12 and enter it on the appropriate line. Other

periodic expenses might include health insurance, contributions to a religious organization, or payment for children's education. Figure out each of these expenses on a *monthly* basis and enter the amounts in the appropriate lines on the Expense Worksheet.

3. Add up the weekly columns to arrive at a total for all your expenses. Write the totals on each line.

RECORD YOUR PLASTIC DEBTS

Now fill out the Credit Card and Charge Card Worksheet in Appendix A. The worksheet is set up like this:

CREDIT CARD AND CHARGE CARD WORKSHEET

CREDIT CARD OR CHARGE CARD	BALANCE	FINANCE CHARGE	MINIMUM PAYMENT

Referring to your most recent statements, enter the name of each card, the full balance that you owe (as of that statement), the finance charge (printed on the statement), and the minimum payment for the most recent month.

At the bottom of the sheet, fill in the total balance, total finance charges, and total minimum payments.

ADD UP YOUR INCOME

Finally, turn to the Income Worksheet in Appendix A. Enter the after-tax earnings for yourself and any other earners in the household. Also list all other sources of earnings—after taxes, on a monthly basis. Then add all your earnings together to arrive at your total net monthly income.

GET THE BOTTOM LINE

Using the Income Worksheet, add up your total monthly expenses and your total credit card minimum payments. Subtract that sum from your monthly income.

You now have your financial profile for one month, and it's time to . . .

Evaluate the Numbers

Typically people react to the results of this one-month financial profile in one of three ways. Either they sit back when it's all done and say "Whew, I didn't know I was spending that much," or they say "How will I ever get out from under that debt?" And a few say "Well, it's not as bad as I thought it was."

There could be many surprises here. But the point is, you don't *know* unless you do a rough profile. And that means considering everything.

Now, as you compare the total monthly payments that you owe (the sum of your monthly expenses plus the minimum payments on your credit cards) with your total household monthly income, it's quite possible that you see an anomaly. And the anomaly is . . . that your payments exceed your income.

If that's the case, welcome to your out-of-checkbook experience!

In fact it's advisable to look upon this as an experience. Pretend that it's not quite happening to you. Casually regard this worksheet as though it belongs to someone else. Say "Hmmm, that's interesting." Take a deep breath. And now go on.

MINUSES AND PLUSES

Nearly all the bad news is over. Everything else, from this point on, is going to be easier.

But let's pause to notice something right here. This financial profile does not reflect your total net worth. If you're a home owner, for instance, the current value of your home may be much more than your outstanding debt. And the loan on a car, or cars, is of course *secured debt*.

Also, right now you don't need to pay much attention to the total debts outstanding, whether secured or unsecured (although this is information you'll want later). What we're now concerned with is the monthly inflow and outflow. And if the outflow exceeds the inflow, that means you're getting deeper in debt every month.

That's the part that can't go on forever.

And if you want to make sure it won't, you can begin by setting some goals.

Establish Your Goals

This is where the action you take begins to make positive changes in your monthly profile. Get out your three worksheets and sit down at the kitchen table. If yours is a household of more than one, get everyone together and explain that you're all going to try to cut down on unnecessary expenses so that you can have more money for what you all want in the future.

Then review each item on the Expense Worksheet line by line. As you review each item, ask:

- Is this a necessary expenditure?
- Is there any way it can be reduced?
- If so, by *how much* can it be reduced?
- What is my (our) goal for this item?

For some items a reduction may not be possible—or realistic. In that case, in the right-hand column of the Expense Worksheet, enter as your goal the same figure as your monthly total. If spending on the item *can* be reduced, enter the new figure in the "Goal" column.

Notice that you're not looking at the total, bottom-line goal as you go line by line through your financial profile. Just concentrate on each item and figure out realistically what your goal is for that particular item.

CAN YOU SEE THE BALLOON ITEMS?

Again, a number of items on your Expense Worksheet can't be changed very much, if at all. Basic necessities such as rent or mortgage, car payments, food bought at the grocery store, insurance premiums, and educational expenses won't change in the near future (unless you move, sell your car, etc.).

So the expenses to look at most closely are the "balloon items"—so called because the money you spend on these items can balloon to many times more than what needs to be spent. Among the typical balloon items are gifts, clothing, luxuries ranging from cars to cameras, expensive lunches and dinners, lavish entertainment, special treats, pricey toys for kids, cosmetics, club memberships, extra furnishings, and that very broad category of what might be called "Toys for Adults."

In all likelihood you won't have to reduce your spending on necessities if you can reduce spending on the balloon items. If the balloons have gotten steadily larger throughout your financial history, it's probably time to shrink them down to more reasonable sizes. Look at each one of them carefully as you set a new goal.

Note: Do not leave the table until you've entered a goal for every expense. You'll need the total of your goals for step 3.

Moving On

During the next few months, continue your financial profile by starting a new Expense Worksheet each month. And continue with the step 1 process: save your receipts,

■
HOW TO RUN A BLAME-FREE BUDGET MEETING

If you're working on your financial profile and setting new goals with your partner or other family members, they may need some gentle guidance to keep this discussion on a positive note. Remember, the goal is not to assign blame for past spending; the goal is to arrive at new goals that you and your partner can live with.

Should the discussion get into pugilistic bartering ("I won't give up this unless you give up that," etc.), here's some guidance for getting it back on track:

- Suggest that both of you first try to set new goals for certain items rather than trying to eliminate them from your budget.
- Make the first offer yourself. ("Well, I think I can cut back on. . . .")
- If something's going to hurt, admit it. ("I hate to pack my own lunch in the morning, but. . . .")
- Leave recommendations in the hands of the "expert." ("You know how much we spend on drugstore items—I don't. Any possibility of cutbacks?")

keep a notebook, and add up your expenses at the end of each week.

There are several reasons for continuing. This is a good way to check on yourself and also an excellent way to refine your financial profile. Can you meet your new goals? Is it possible to find *more* savings by deflating some balloon items?

You'll also have the reward of self-satisfaction if you continue the profile. When you start cutting expenses, reducing your spending, and meeting goals, that will show up clearly on the Expense Worksheet. It's very satisfying to know that you can reach the financial goals that you set for yourself.

And since you *can* reach those goals, you're ready for the next step: you're ready to lock up your credit cards.

S T E P **1** **R E V I E W**

1. Keep track of your daily expenses by collecting receipts and recording expenses in a notebook.

2. Add up the household's expenses in each category and record each week's totals on the Expense Worksheet.

3. Total the expenses in each category at the end of the month. Be sure to record payments for rent, utilities, and the like, plus the one-month portion of periodic expenses.

4. Record your minimum monthly payments on the Credit Card and Charge Card Worksheet.

5. Record the monthly income of the household on the Income Worksheet.

6. Subtract your total monthly expenses and credit payments from your income.

7. Review your Expense Worksheet and set goals for each item.

You now have a complete one-month financial profile—what you earned and what you spent for one month—and a plan for changing that profile for the better.

LOCK UP YOUR CREDIT CARDS

▪ ▪

You should now be fully prepared to lock up your credit cards and charge cards.

They don't have to stay locked up forever. You don't have to cut them into tiny little pieces or throw away the key to the drawer.

But if step 1 showed you that your monthly expenses exceed your monthly income, locking up the cards is the very next step in your inexorable march toward financial security.

There are two reasons for this action step:

1. You don't need credit cards.
2. Every month that goes by that you have a balance due, you're being ripped off!

You may not agree with point 1.

Point 2—well, deep in your heart, you *know* it's true. Interest rates like 16, 19.8, 24 percent, and higher are *outrageous*. What we're going to do here is give you permission to be outraged, as you have a right to be—and then a way to do something about it.

Take Action

1. Lock up all your credit cards—in a desk drawer, a safe deposit box, or wherever they will be inaccessible. *How* accessible you need to make them depends on how strong you think temptation will be.

2. If you have business expenses, keep *one* card, for business use only. *Absolutely no personal expenses on your business card!*

Who Says You Need Credit Cards?

Let's look at point 1 first, because most of us have our inner game of risk. And central to that game is "110 Reasons Why I Must Have Credit Cards to Survive."

To conquer the plastic habit, you require positive empirical evidence that you don't need those cards. In other words you have to start living without them *immediately*.

You're going to prove that to yourself by doing it.

But first, let's look at why you're using credit cards.

For most people there are two main areas of use—personal and business. Plus there's a fuzzy gray area of credit card use that lies somewhere in between.

FOR PERSONAL USE

In the personal category you probably use credit cards for all, some, or a few of the following purposes:

- Buying clothing
- Eating out

- Drinking
- Theater, concert, sports event tickets
- Sports and recreation (golf? skiing? racquetball? tennis?)
- Memberships
- Gas, car repairs
- Furniture
- Appliances
- Gadgets
- Gifts
- Books, records, CDs, tapes
- Car rental
- Transportation fare
- Hotel/motel/lodge/inn accommodations

"GETTING TO YES" WITH YOUR PARTNER

If you're married or living together, locking up the cards may require a bit of discussion. Mutual agreement is essential. If either one of you continues to use a card or two, it does more than hurt your budget—it's also unfair to the partner who has locked up his or her cards.

Those pieces of plastic mean many things to many people—not only buying power but also freedom, luxury, prosperity, and independence. If your partner finds the whole idea hard to swallow, listen to what he or she has to say. Like other steps of the action plan, this has to be something that you both do together.

Borrowing from Roger Fisher and William Ury of the Harvard Negotiation Project,* we strongly recommend one of their tips for these difficult times: *Separate the person from the problem.*

In other words, when you're negotiating, remember it's not your fault that you're overextended on your credit cards. It's not your partner's fault either. But it's a problem—quite possibly your biggest financial problem. By focusing on the problem itself and not blaming yourself or your partner for overusing the cards, you're much more likely to reach mutual agreement to lock them up.

*Getting to YES: Negotiating Agreement Without Giving In, Penguin, 1981.

Granted, if you lock up your cards, you might have to exist without some of these things. Can you do it?

What's going to happen now that you have only one card and you can use it only for business expenses? Will the consequences be so terrible?

The chances are, you pay by check or cash when you go grocery shopping. So, even without your credit card you can still eat. Also, you undoubtedly have sufficient cash for transportation to and from work, whether you drive or take public transportation. You don't need credit for that. And since you're not paying your rent or mortgage with a credit card, you still have a place to live even if you lock up the plastic.

Logical conclusion: Even though you've locked up all your personal credit cards, you still have all the fundamentals you need for the next month—food, transportation, and shelter.

How to Survive Austerity

Okay, now let's look at what you'll have to do without now that you've locked up the cards. (This is the nasty part—but be patient, it's not really as nasty as you might think.)

Clothing. Open your closet. Look inside. Can you get by with what you have for a month, at least? (You know you can.)

Eating out. Okay, this may hurt. It's really nice to go to a great restaurant, be waited on, have a wonderful meal. If this is one of your greatest pleasures in life, we'll help you plan on getting it back again. But not at dire cost! Not on a credit card! For an interim period you'll probably have to forgo fancy, overpriced food.

Drinking. Okay, but not on your credit card. If you miss the companionship that goes with drinking, invite some friends over and split the cost of the beverages. Using cash, of course.

Theater, concert, sports event tickets. Sorry, they're expensive. If you've been buying them on credit in the past, this is the month to give up that habit.

Sports and recreation. If you have a club membership that's paid for, this is the month to enjoy as many of the free facilities as possible. If you have to pay for courts, pool, workout room, or other facilities, start paying for those things with a check or cash.

Memberships. If they aren't paid for yet, see if your membership dues can ride for a month or two while you're getting this debt situation straightened out. If not, let them lapse.

Gas, car repairs. Pay cash for gas. If you get into some steep car repairs this month, go to extraordinary lengths to avoid whipping out your plastic. If you have any kind of savings account or emergency fund, use that to pay for your car repairs. If you don't, it's advisable to consider cutting out *all* unnecessary expenses so you can pay the car repair bill. Needless to say, you need your transportation. But for your own financial sanity you also need to keep your credit cards locked up. Only under conditions of the most extreme necessity should you unlock the *one* card you *might* need to pay for car repairs. And then write a check as soon as possible to cover the charges you run up.

Furniture. Do you have a bed? A table? Chairs? Then you don't need any new furniture this month.

Appliances. Got a stove? Refrigerator? You'll make it.

Gadgets. Of course it would be fun to get a new pocket calculator that keeps your grocery list, brushes your teeth, and pays tolls for you—but do you really need it this month? Whatever the gadget you have your eye on, let some time go by. That way you'll find out whether your gadget-grabbing impulse remains strong and lasting. If it does, you'll probably be able to purchase the same coveted, silicon-chip gadget for half the price sometime in the near future.

Books, records, CDs, tapes. You have a library. You have

a radio. You probably have a stereo and a few records, tapes, or CDs on hand. You'll get by this month.

Tools. Borrow from a friend. Get to know your neighbors.

Gifts. Be reasonable. Pay cash. Send cards. It's the thought that counts. Any friend or relative who *demands* lavish gifts is not a friend or relative you need to nurture right now.

Car rental. This could be a problem. If you absolutely need to rent a car, the easiest way to do it is with a credit card. (There are ways to pay cash, but we can't pretend the hassle is worth going through.) However, before you get out your plastic for this expense, be excruciatingly honest with yourself. Is this trip *really* necessary this month? Can't you take a train or bus and pay cash? Can't you find a friend who has a car?

For this expense, and *this one only,* you can use a credit card, but with one important proviso. As soon as you return the car and get the bill, write out a check for the full amount and mail it in to your credit card account. *Then lock up the card again.*

If you can't afford to do that, then you can't afford to rent that car.

Transportation fare. Either you pay cash, you put the expenses on your business card (if it's a bona fide business expense), or you hang around home this month. No credit card–based deposits on future vacation trips. (In step 5 you'll start to plan your pleasures.) Even a once-in-a-lifetime vacation opportunity comes up more than once in a lifetime (in some other form). And no vacation on a credit card is worth the postvacation, try-to-pay-for-it stress.

FOR BUSINESS USE

You've kept one card, and it's for business expenses only. That's fine—it's much easier to pay for business expenses with plastic than to haul around a lot of cash.

And every dollar and every penny should be completely reimbursed by your employer. (If you're self-employed, reimbursement comes promptly at the end of every month from your *separate business account*.)

If you work for a company that has an unclear policy about all this, it's advisable to schedule a meeting with some individual who can clarify the policy so you know what's allowable and get reimbursed promptly and fully. If there seems to be negotiation over expense items every time you turn in your report, receipts, or vouchers, meet with someone who can *establish* policy and then keep that person informed. You simply can't afford to cover business expenses using your personal funds.

■

DO YOU NEED NEW CREDIT CARD OFFERS?

No, of course not. But on the other hand, it's nice to be asked.

If you are paying off the balance on your unused cards, new offers will probably keep coming in the mail.

We all know what those form letters look like.

"Dear Friend," a typical offer begins, "what do you call a credit card that *gives you more and saves you money too*?"

Right away there's a certain wording here that should set off alarm bells. First of all, what kind of friend is it who regularly lends at 19.8 percent interest? (Take a look at the reverse side of the come-on. By law that application has to indicate the annual percentage rate for purchases. And if this credit card offer is like most of them, that rate is probably above 18 percent and is most likely to be around 20 or 21 percent.) Second, there's something peculiar about a card that gives and saves all in the same breath.

That letter from your friend should go straight into your local recycling center. After that it will be turned into useful pulp.

As your financial situation improves, you'll get more of those letters. There's no law against sending you such an offer.

And no law against throwing it away.

THE FUZZY GRAY AREA

Where trouble creeps in is when you put personal and business expenses on the same card. That's the dangerous gray area. So how do you deal with it now?

You don't. There *is* no fuzzy gray area for you anymore. You pay for personal necessities with cash (or check), and you have one credit card for business expenses only. Period.

Looking Ahead

You may wonder when you'll be able to unlock your cards. The answer is not quite "never," but close to it.

And there are fringe benefits . . .

First, when you stop using your credit card, you *never* have to worry about mistakes on your monthly credit card bills. If you have a lot of cards and you haven't been checking carefully over the years, there's a chance you paid some charges that you didn't incur. Now *any* new charges that show up are a mistake. All you have to do is call the 800 number listed on the bill, point out the error, and follow up with a brief letter explaining why the statement is incorrect. It's up to the credit card company to trace the bill—and once you've challenged it in writing, the company can't charge interest on the amount in dispute.

Second, after many months of not using your credit cards—or after they're all paid off—you'll be likely to receive a notice in the mail that says "Congratulations! As one of our most valued customers, your credit line has been increased." You can now take satisfaction in knowing that your credit record is improving all the time even though you aren't using the card anymore. Your locked-up cards are earning creditworthiness for you.

S T E P 2 R E V I E W

1. Lock up all your credit cards . . .

2. . . . except for one for business expenses only.

3. For a crucial car repair or personal-use car rental, you may unlock one card *only* if you can write a check and send it to the credit card company immediately. Then lock up the card again.

You no longer have to worry about those credit card bills growing each month, and now you're ready to learn to pay as you go.

PREPARE THE LUMP-SUM, TINKER-PROOF, GET-THROUGH-THE-WEEK, DON'T-FOOL-YOURSELF BUDGET PLAN

■ ■

Once you lock up your cards, budgeting becomes magnificently simplified. Why? Because there's only one way you can get through each month, and that's to pay as you go.

The Lump-Sum, Tinker-Proof, Get-Through-the-Week, Don't-Fool-Yourself Budget Plan begins as soon as you lock up your credit cards. Here's how it works:

On the lump-sum plan you simply use cash to pay for all your necessary and usual weekly expenditures. For this plan what we're calling "weekly expenses" include the following.

• *The basic grocery bill.* This does not, of course, include dining out or buying gourmet foods every time you shop. It's just the normal amount you spend every week—without scrimping but without overspending.

• *Transportation expenses.* If you own a car, then this is the cost of gas and tolls. If you're commuting or using public transportation, it would be the price of tickets and fares.

• *Entertainment.* On the lump-sum plan you're paying for all your entertainment in cash—no credit cards! Look at the monthly goal you arrived at for the entertainment items on your Expense Worksheet. What *is* your goal for entertainment expenses? Divide it by four to see how much you intend to spend on entertainment every week.

• *Necessities for you.* Of course you'll need to buy toothpaste, home maintenance items, and other necessities from time to time. Check your Expense Worksheet and see how much you've spent on these items in the past. Is your goal for these items any less? Set aside the target amount.

(Of course there's no hard and fast rule here about what constitutes a necessity. What's necessary to one person may seem highly frivolous to another. On the other hand, there's a simple test: If you don't get this item now, will it be *necessary* for you to buy it at some time in the future? If the answer is no, then in all likelihood you don't need it right now either.)

• *Necessities for children.* If you have children, other expenses for them need to be anticipated in your weekly cash budget. These include weekly cost of (necessary) baby-sitting or child care, allowances, lunch money, and other necessities (check your Expense Worksheet).

Drawing Up Your Plan

With the expense goals you set in step 1 you have all the data you need to draw up your budget in less than an hour.

1. Calculate the cash. Use the Budget Worksheet in Appendix B to figure out how much you need *in cash* each week. Referring to your Expense Worksheet, first decide which items are cash expenses; those you can pay for in cash versus those you must customarily write a check for (such as a utility bill). Circle YES on the Budget Worksheet for the ones that are cash expenses. Then fill in the monthly goal that you determined for each of those items and enter that amount in the right-hand column.

On the final page, add up all the right-hand-column figures to find out how much cash you need for the month. Then divide by four to get a weekly figure.

Here's what the worksheet looks like:

BUDGET WORKSHEET FOR ACTION STEP 3

EXPENSE	CASH EXPENSE? (YES/NO)	MONTHLY GOAL FOR THIS ITEM
[Expense item]	Yes No	$_____

---

2. If you have a one-person household, you're all set to put the plan into action. You've determined a total cash amount for every week. And that's really all you need. As long as that amount of cash is all you carry in your wallet, that's all you can spend. That's why the lump-sum approach guarantees that you don't overspend.

If you have a spouse or partner and you are both working, each of you can decide how much cash each of you will need to get through the week. Transportation can be figured out separately, but you'll need to confer about shared food bills, necessities that you buy for the household, and the shared entertainment bill.

If one of you customarily buys groceries and necessities, whoever is doing the buying gets the cash. But it's important that you both agree on the amounts you're going to spend.

Young children don't need to be participants in the plan, of course, though they should certainly be told about it. If you're asking them to begin saving their own money or to defer toy buying that used to be frequent, they should know why.

If you have older children who get a regular allowance, they need to live under the same rules. Whatever they get at the beginning of the week needs to last until the end. (Of course you might give them the option of earning and saving on their own.) If they've been coming to you to plea-bargain for money, and getting it, this new program is going to force a change in their style. But perhaps that change was due.

Using the Budget

1. Choose one day of the week on which to withdraw your budgeted amount from the bank. *It's essential that you make only one cash withdrawal from the bank every week.* Since your weekly cash allotment is enough to cover exactly seven days, that means if you draw out money on Friday evening, you have enough to cover you until *next* Friday evening. If more than one of you gets money, dole it out immediately.

2. If you find yourself overspending early in the week and coming up short at the end of the week, you need to go on a stricter plan. Put the weekly cash in a desk drawer at home. Draw out exactly one-seventh of it every morning.

3. If you get to day seven and you still have money for a couple more days, you may be tempted to use your extra cash to cover those days. Don't do it. Put the extra in an envelope marked "Leftovers." (We have great plans for that

extra cash in step 5—but right now, put it aside.) If you've put yourself on the day-by-day plan, stash your leftovers at the end of each day.

4. If the burden of the household purchasing is on one person, confer at the end of each week to find out how things are going.

Here's Why It Works

Something remarkable happens when you go on this cash budget.

Survival instincts take over.

For instance, on any given day, if you know you have only enough in your wallet to buy a tank of gas, and you won't be able to drive for the rest of the week until you fill the tank, guess what you'll spend the money on? The gas!

Why?

Well, let's say on the way home from work you pass by Café Cherie Cher, which has a Cinq-Etoile take-out dinner special for 18 times the price of a hot dog. You're tempted. Very tempted. It's been a long, hard day, and you deserve something special for your palate.

A trivial example?

Not at all.

This is exactly the kind of thing the Lump-Sum, Tinker-Proof, Get-Through-the-Week, Don't-Fool-Yourself Budget Plan can do for you. It simplifies what used to be astronomically complex calculations involving lines of credit and electronic transfers and turns you into a creature of necessity, immune to financial abstractions. To illustrate this, compare "logical thinking" under the two systems.

THINKING UNDER THE OLD-MATH SYSTEM

"It's been a rough day. I feel like buying something. I know that Cinq-Etoile take-out special *is* something special. Trouble is, I've got only enough in my pocket to pay for gas. Well, I can pay cash for the Cinq-Etoile and use my Gulf Card for gas. Or I can pay cash for gas and use a credit card at Café Cherie Cher. But which credit card? Maybe I can get away with making this a business expense. No, it'll never get by. Well, it's personal then. But I hate to put more on my card. It's already 90 days overdue. Maybe I can use the bank machine. But I don't know what my balance is at the bank. Well, I know approximately. I'm sure I can take out enough to pay cash for the gas, the croissants, plus some spending money. Now where's the nearest machine? But wait a minute . . . what if I use my *credit card* in the machine? Then I can take out cash to cover all this, and some for next week too, and when my salary clears, I'll just do a phone transfer from checking to the credit card. Last time I forgot to do that. But this time . . ."

THINKING UNDER THE NEW-MATH SYSTEM

"If I buy the Cinq-Etoile special, I go without gas. If I go without gas, I don't get to work the rest of the week. Ergo, I'll forgo the special. I'll pay for the gas."

A bit brutal, yes.

Some law of the jungle here.

But it works every time.

Watching Out for the Pitfalls

If you let this plan work for you, it will come through. But beware the snares.

"JUST A FEW DOLLARS MORE"

If you start taking out just a little extra to cover who-knows-what, the system will start to break down. You might find yourself on day five with only enough cash to squeak by on day seven. In that case it's all too easy to panic and hit the bank machine for a few 20s just to get you through. Don't do it.

SPENDING WITH FRIENDS

As your spending habits change under the lump-sum system, you may find that some of your socializing habits also change.

When we're socializing, we tend to spend what those around us are spending. After all, we need to pay our part of the tab. Sometimes, in fact, we feel almost morally obligated to outdo our friends' generosity. So if we're with speed-spenders, we're likely to move at their pace. We acquire some of their habits and reach excesses of expenditure that we wouldn't have believed possible.

The question is, if we no longer have access to a seemingly infinite line of electronic money, will our friends still be our friends?

There's one quick way to find out. Let them know what's happening in your financial life. Let them know that you're on a cash-only basis for the foreseeable future.

They don't need all the details, of course. But there's no reason why real friends shouldn't know that you're overindebted, that your anxiety level is at an all-time high, and that you're trying to get your finances under control. In fact they may admit (with a sigh of relief) that they have a similar "confession" to make. That frees you *and* your friends to look for some cheaper alternatives.

There's another kind of social pressure as well. When someone calls about subscription tickets or a money-raising event, the heat is on (even if it's a "soft sell"). But it's perfectly okay to say you're watching your budget and you just can't contribute this time. That's the truth—and you have no reason to be embarrassed about it. If the event, extravaganza, or outing is something that you never want to miss again, start saving for it in your Plan Your Pleasures Account (step 5).

Your Newfound Budget Power

Although the lump-sum budget plan may seem restrictive at first, you will discover that it actually gives you one great freedom—freedom from worry. When you know you can spend what's in your wallet without going further into debt, you'll probably find that you are a lot more comfortable with spending, because there won't be any retribution (in the form of unpaid bills) later on.

And when you know you can stick to a spending plan, that gives you a lot more confidence in managing your budget. Additional confidence will come in handy when you take the next important step—negotiating with your creditors.

STEP 3 REVIEW

1. Pull your cash expense items from the Expense Worksheet and list the goal amounts for them on the Budget Worksheet.

2. Add up the monthly cash amounts and divide by four to get a weekly budget total.

3. Decide who will purchase which household items and calculate who gets what portion of the weekly cash.

4. Go to the bank once a week to withdraw the household's budget amount. Divide up the money among family members.

5. If you're running short before the end of the week, put yourself on the day-by-day plan.

6. At the end of each week (or day), put extra cash in a "Leftovers" envelope.

You now see that you don't need credit cards, that you can honestly evaluate where you need to spend your money, and that you can even end up with money left over.

NEGOTIATE WITH YOUR CREDITORS

Okay, you came up with a financial profile (step 1). You locked up your cards (step 2). You've just started on the lump-sum weekly budget plan (step 3).

Now let's take a look at that pile of bills in your drawer and figure out what you can do about them.

First of all, you may already be in much better financial shape just because you implemented the first three steps of this action plan. When you started your financial profile, you probably began paying more attention to balloon items—and deflating them. As soon as you locked up your cards, you guaranteed that you wouldn't be adding any new charges to those cards. So you may already be saving enough money to meet all your monthly bills.

But what if you aren't?

First of all, you need to determine how much you can pay on your credit cards and charge cards after . . .

1. You've paid the bills for your monthly necessities; and
2. You've set aside money to meet your weekly expenses.

To accomplish that, turn to Appendix C.

Calculate How Much You Can Pay

The worksheet in Appendix C will allow you to calculate how much money you have for credit card and charge card payments when you are meeting your monthly budget goals. This is information you urgently need before you can begin negotiating with your creditors. That is, you need to know your bargaining position—how much you can actually afford to pay every month and still meet your other expenses.

1. Following the instructions on this worksheet, subtract your total monthly expense goals (Expense Worksheet) from your total monthly income (Income Worksheet). This shows what you *can* pay to creditors each month.

2. From what you *can* pay, subtract your total minimum monthly credit payments (Credit Card and Charge Card Worksheet). This gives the excess or shortage.

If the figure you get is a negative number, you know you can't meet your minimum credit card payments even if you are meeting your optimum spending goals every month. You will have to negotiate with your creditors to get them to accept payments that are less than the minimum amounts.

Example

Suppose your total monthly take-home income
(line A on the step 4 Worksheet) is $2,500

Suppose your total monthly expenses—your new
  goal (line B) are $2,000
Subtracting line B from line A, you get line C . . . . $ 500
And . . .
Your total minimum credit card/charge card
  payments (line D) are . . . . $ 650
Subtracting line D from line C, you get (line E) . . ⟨$ 150⟩

That is, minus $150.

In other words, you will be $150 short each month. So you will have to negotiate with your creditors to reduce your monthly payments by $150.

If line E is a positive number—that is, you have an excess—go directly to step 5.

Your Negotiating Position: Be Prepared

Before you begin actual negotiations, review your own position—and consider the position of the people you're going to negotiate with. Don't pick up the phone until you have a firm proposal to offer your creditors. Remember, this action plan is designed to put *you* in control of your finances, not to leave you at the mercy of your creditors.

For the sake of illustration, let's assume you've been paying the minimum on your Boundforglory Card to BFG Bank for the past three years. But you've also been running up new charges now and then. So your average balance for these years has been a steady $2,000.

If BFG has charged 19 percent annual interest, that means the bank has made $380 in each of those years. In other words, BFG has already made $1,140 off you—and you *still* owe the bank $2,000.

Now what happens if you suddenly decide you can't pay anything at all? The producers of the plastic will send you dunning notices that become increasingly authoritative. And the final vitriolic message will inform you that

BFG is turning your account over to Swiftsword Collection Agency.

That's supposed to intimidate you into submission.

But the interesting thing is: the credit card company doesn't really want to resort to such extreme measures!

WHY YOUR CREDITOR STILL WANTS YOU

Here's the reason: A collection agency gets a whopping commission (up to 40 percent) on everything it collects. Then it pays the balance to the lending institution. That means that if the agency squeezes the full $2,000 out of you, the credit card company may get only 60 percent of the total, or $1,200. Put that together with the $1,140 you've already paid in interest, and the credit card company gets only $340 in profit for loaning you $2,000 for three years! That kind of return on investment doesn't even count as real money.

What's more, the actual picture for BFG may be even gloomier. One common characteristic of collection agencies is that they like to close their deals fast. So Swiftsword may be willing to settle for less than the full amount—in fact, it may *have* to. Collection agencies recognize that the reason honest people don't pay is usually that they *can't* pay—they simply don't have the money. And Swiftsword has had a lot of hands-on experience trying to squeeze water from stone.

So, after much *sturm und drang* through the mail and over the phone, Swiftsword Collection Agency may agree to accept payment of $1,000 instead of the full $2,000. The agency takes 40 percent and sends 60 percent to BFG.

That means BFG collects only $600 out of the $2,000 you owe! Put that together with the $1,140 you paid in interest, and BFG's income is a measly $1,740. In other words, by turning your account over to a collection agency the credit card company runs the risk of losing $260 on the $2,000 it loaned you for three years.

(And not so incidentally, there are all kinds of things a creditor and/or a collection agency *can't* do to collect the money—like harassing you with phone calls, seizing your car and house, or contacting your employer. For your rights in these situations, see "Tactic 1: Dealing with Collection Agencies" in Part II.)

WHO GETS WHAT?

The problem now is to figure out how to divide what you can pay among all those who *want* you to pay. You can assume that they all want you to pay the minimum amount—that anything less is considered insufficient. So if you're going to negotiate and come to terms with these companies, you first need to come up with an alternative plan. Then you have to figure out how much you intend to pay each one.

Depending on your situation, there may be many credit card companies you need to negotiate with or just a few. The important thing is to consider every debt negotiable. Just because it's printed out by a computer and sent to you through the U.S. mail doesn't mean that amount is authorized by the Almighty or fixed in stone. It's true that a company can try to collect or cancel your card if you fail to make a minimum payment. But nearly always, you *can* negotiate, even if your creditors try to convince you otherwise.

WHAT DOES *MINIMUM* REALLY MEAN?

In your agreement with the credit card issuer—probably in very fine print—there's a somewhat complicated formula for determining the "minimum due" on each bill. But if you can't pay that amount, does that mean you shouldn't pay anything at all?

Of course not. It stands to reason the issuer of the card would rather have you pay something than nothing. The question is how much that "something" is going to be. And that's where the negotiations come in.

To simplify, let's suppose you have four credit cards,

each with an outstanding balance of $1,500, and your "minimum payment" on each card is $75. If you were able to meet your payments on all the cards, you would pay a total of $300 at the end of the month.

Now, let's further suppose that you don't have $300 available for credit card payments. After you finish with the worksheet in Appendix C, you realize you'll have only $150 available each month with which to pay your credit cards. What can you do?

Let's look at a few alternatives:

Alternative 1

Pay the full minimum to companies 1 and 2 and pay nothing to 3 and 4.

Alternative 2

Use your line of credit from card 1 to get cash advance and use that advance to pay off cards 2, 3, and 4.

Alternative 3

Pay one quarter of $150.00 (that is, $37.50) to each of the four companies.

If you had to choose one alternative, which would it be? Well, let's look at the pros and cons.

Alternative 1

If you decide not to pay anything to companies 3 and 4, they're likely to get very insistent very soon. They may end up turning your account over to a collection agency. However, they're much more likely to be cooperative if you make some effort to pay, even if the amount is less than they ask for. So let's assume that alternative 1 isn't practical.

Alternative 2

If you have a $6,000 line of credit with company 1, and you're using only $1,500 of it, why not take a cash advance from card 1 and use those advances to pay off companies 2, 3, and 4?

The main drawback is that credit card companies charge higher interest for cash advances. For instance, a company that charges 19.8 percent on purchases is likely to charge a ferocious 24 percent on cash advances. As a result you would end up paying more interest just for consolidating all your outstanding balances on one card.

■ **INTEREST, INTEREST**

The only hitch, no matter which bargaining alternative you choose, is that you'll have to continue paying interest on the unpaid balance. And you'll end up paying *more* interest than you would if you could meet the minimum payments. In effect what you're doing is called *stretching out* the loan. The credit card company will have to wait longer to get its principal repaid, but in return it will be earning more interest.

To find out what the interest is, look at the "finance charge" part of your bill. If the annual percentage rate is 19.8 percent, then the periodic rate (the rate for each month) is 1.65 percent. How does this translate?

Well, if you owe $1,500, the finance charge will be $24.75 for the month.

So, if you decide to pay $37.50 a month to the credit card company, you'll be paying $24.75 in interest and $12.75 on the principal. Granted, it will take you a long time to pay it off at this rate. But at least you're paying all the interest as well as *something* on the principal, and as you pay off the principal, eventually you'll be paying less interest.

Alternative 3

This alternative has a lot to recommend it. You're paying *something* on each account, and you're dealing with companies 1, 2, 3, and 4 on equal terms. There's a drawback in that you have to negotiate with all the companies. But you're certainly being evenhanded.

So alternative 3 is probably the best approach. This means your goal for step 4 is to negotiate with the four companies to get them each to accept your payments of $37.50.

GET READY

Realistically, you have to assume that the representative of Boundforglory Credit Card is not going to be delighted to hear you make this proposal. Be prepared to hear someone sternly remind you that you agreed to certain terms at the time you were issued the card. The BFG representative may also threaten to turn your account over to a collection agency or subject you to legal action.

All this may be true—but keep in mind that you have a few arguments on your side.

Open Negotiations

1. On your bill there's an 800 number. This is a good place to start. However, the person on the other end of the line will probably *not* make a decision about your proposal, much less offer a counterproposal. Just tell that person that you can't pay the full minimum and you want to speak to someone about arranging a repayment plan. You'll undoubtedly be referred to someone in a position of "higher authority."

2. When the "authority" comes on the line, ask

whether the person to whom you are speaking can make a decision on your account. If he or she answers in the affirmative, describe your plan:

- Explain your situation. Tell the authority that you are overindebted and that you are trying in good faith to meet your obligations fairly. Let the person who's handling your account know that you've conscientiously worked out a repayment schedule and you'd like to stretch out the loan so you can pay it off in full.

- Name your figure. If the company accepts your repayment proposal, you promise to pay promptly on a specified day every month. Emphasize that your payments will always be on time and that you will send your payments to the attention of the higher authority to whom you are speaking.

- Stress the upside. The amount you propose is a minimum. Should your financial situation improve, you will notify the company and increase your monthly payments. And if the company accepts this plan, you will eventually pay the outstanding balance in full. (You don't need to say how soon—the authority can work that out.)

- Reiterate your good intentions. The payment plan that you're proposing should allow you to remain financially solvent, which is your creditor's best opportunity of receiving full repayment in the long run. Not only that, but you have stopped using the card, and you don't intend to use it anymore until your financial situation changes. (You don't need to go into lengthy detail.)

You have just presented an extremely well-reasoned case in a very rational tone of voice. But what if the higher authority begins to argue with you? What if he or she absolutely refuses to agree to your terms? You can still get your point across using sheer persistence:

3. As soon as you get off the phone, write a letter addressed to the authority, restating your intention to pay a specified amount by a specified day every month. Enclose your first month's payment.

4. Stick to your plan. Of course you will probably continue to receive the standard notices telling you that your payments are overdue, and yes, the creditor *might* turn your account over to a collection agency. But remember all the reasons the creditor is disinclined to take that action and that this is *your* plan that *you've* worked out for financial solvency. If you give in to the hysterical demands of this creditor, some other bill will have to go unpaid. Meanwhile, persistence is your best argument. Pay as you promised, on time, every month. Also stick to your promise to reevaluate your situation when you get a substantial salary increase or when some other account is paid off.

■

PARALLEL NEGOTIATING

If you and your spouse or partner both want to negotiate with creditors, you will be more effective if you "assign" some accounts to yourself and some to your partner. Discuss with each other what's going on, but handle the calls and the correspondence separately. In other words, if you have four creditors who are trying to collect, you take the calls from Nag Department Store and Crunch Collection Agency and let your spouse or partner handle the Glint Credit and Savant Club Dining accounts.

If both of you try to handle all the accounts, the caller might get you to agree to some terms that your spouse wouldn't, or vice versa. Also, your success may depend on the over-the-phone relationship you develop with the representative of the company.

Once you have divided up the account duties, don't handle any calls from a company that your partner is handling. Simply tell the representative that your partner will respond to the call or ask the representative to call back at another time.

Winning Through Persistence

In most instances, if you stick to your plan, you'll get your way.

Despite sending you notices, your creditor is likely to accept payments on your terms because it's ultimately in the company's best interest to do so.

When you *can* increase payments, write directly to the officer you spoke to previously, informing that individual of your intent to increase your monthly payments.

You may get no reply at all, but the satisfaction of paying off this credit line will be enormous.

(And in the meantime—keep those credit cards locked up!)

Credit Counseling

If you decide that you don't want to negotiate directly with creditors, you can turn to a credit counselor who will do the negotiation for you—either for free or for a small fee. For more information about credit counseling services, see Part III, "Resource 2: Credit Counseling."

Negotiating with Other Creditors

For specific tactics for negotiating with other creditors, including collection agencies, the IRS (and other tax authorities), utility companies, landlords, banks and mortgage holders, see Part II, "Special Tactics for Tough Times."

Looking Forward to Zero Balance

When you have negotiated with your creditors and begun to make regular payments, your debt should be under control. Now you don't have to dread any unpleasant surprises when you open your next statement or bill. By staying with the plan, you can look forward to the day when the minimum payment due on every bill is "$0.00."

For anyone who has lain awake at night worrying about how to pay the bills, "0.00" is the most beautiful number in the world.

S T E P 4 R E V I E W

1. Calculate how much you can pay your creditors, using the worksheet in Appendix C.

2. Prepare your proposal: understand your bargaining position, decide how much to pay which creditors, and get ready to make some calls.

3. Call your creditor and locate a "higher authority."

4. Once you've found the appropriate officer, explain your situation, lay out your proposal, and be positive—about your own intentions and the benefits the company will glean from accepting your plan.

5. Whether your proposal is accepted or not, follow up the phone calls with letters restating your position; enclose a check for the amount of your new "minimum" payment.

6. Do what you promised to do—pay what you agreed to, on time, every month.

7. When you find more income at your disposal, write to each company to announce that you will be increasing your payments.

You have taken back control of your financial life and are on the way to reaping some rewards.

STEP 5 • • • • •

GET BACK TO THE FUTURE

• •

Since you began using the lump-sum budget, it's quite possible that you made a surprising discovery: After you used your cash for the week, you still had money left over.

That's the money you put in your "Leftovers" envelope.

But there's other money that may come in unexpectedly, from a source that you didn't list in your financial profile. Some unanticipated sources might be gifts, bonuses, tax refunds, repayment of debts owed to you, or income from part-time work.

The question is, when you find yourself with leftover end-of-the-month money, what should you do? Allocate a bit more to each of your credit card accounts? Spend a little bit more dining out? Put it into an emergency fund for a rainy day?

Any of those approaches would be virtuous and commendable. But what most of us need for motivation is something quite different from virtue and commendability. We need a simple, safe, effective means of saving for specific goals.

The Three Accounts

The fact is, you need money not only to meet your necessities but also to plan for entertainment, vacations, and future necessities. If you have children—or if you are planning to start a family—you know that planning for their needs and their education is a very big part of your future.

Instead of putting these "found" resources back into the home budget and spreading them among necessity items, the best policy is to divide this money into separate accounts with specific purposes.

First we'll describe exactly what we have in mind for each of those accounts; then we'll tell you what action to take for step 5.

ACCOUNT 1: THE PLAN YOUR PLEASURES (PYP) ACCOUNT

The money you put in this account will be saved for only a few months. Then you will spend it on yourself or with others in your household—just for entertainment and enjoyment. In other words, these small savings are meant to provide you with some rewards in the form of little pleasures in the near future.

What *kinds* of pleasures? Your choice depends on the amount you can put away each week. If you have only $10 a week to sock away, and what you want is a vacation in Cancun, that sun-dappled goal may be such a distant dream that you get discouraged and demotivated. On the other hand, $10 a week could get you a really splendid meal at a four-star restaurant after not-too-many months of saving.

So, here are criteria for the reachable pleasure you're saving for in your PYP Account:

1. It has to be something you really enjoy doing.
2. If it's a purchase, it has to be something that will give you some lasting pride of ownership—more than an impulse buy.
3. It has to be attainable within three months.
4. It has to be paid for *exclusively* from the Plan Your Pleasures Account.

ACCOUNT 2: THE GIFT ACCOUNT

Both the size and the term of the account are variable. Your goal is to put enough in this account to cover your expected expenditures for birthday gifts, wedding presents, holiday gifts, and so on. It's your "insurance policy" so you don't get caught short when these occasions come up.

ACCOUNT 3: THE BIG PLANS (BP) ACCOUNT

This is money that you save for some future goal. That goal could be tuition for you, your partner, or your children. It could be a down payment on a house or car. Or it might be for pleasures that the PYP Account won't cover—that week in Cancun, for instance. The cash that you put in this account can accumulate for quite a long time—and when you pull it out, it will be for something *big* that was worth saving for.

Suppose you *do* want that vacation in Cancun, but you know it will seem to take forever for your PYP Account to cover it. You're beginning to think about using credit again—and you *know* you don't want to do that. So, what do you do?

Alternative 1: Defer your short-term pleasures so you can save for the Big One?

Alternative 2: Wait until everything else is paid off before you allow yourself to start dreaming about the big one?

Alternative 3: Start another account?

The best choice is alternative 3. A moment's reflection will tell you why. Once you've gotten into the habit of paying for your short-term pleasures from your PYP Account, you don't want to start *depriving* yourself in the short term to reward yourself in the long term. That's only a temptation to revert to your line-of-credit activities. But if you start saving for Cancun in your BP Account, you'll be able to enjoy pleasures that are both immediate and somewhat far off.

Start Planning

THE SAVING

1. Using the money in your "Leftovers" envelope from step 3, start a short-term PYP Account and a Gift Account. Each week, strive to add something to each. Ideally you will be able to contribute to these accounts, without fail, on a weekly basis (on the same day of the week if possible). How much you put into each account is up to you and depends, for example, on whether you have umpteen relatives who are all used to getting birthday gifts from you.

2. As soon as you have more than a few dollars in each account, you'll want to get that money into the bank, where it will earn some interest.

However, don't mix the money for these two accounts with your checking account. Start a new savings account—or use an account that's been inactive—to build up your PYP and gift reserves.

There are sound psychological reasons for this. If you put this money in your regular checking account—even if you know exactly how much you're putting in every month—you're likely to spend it on other things.

You'll be drawing most of the money out of the PYP Account within the next few months, and you'll probably be tapping the Gift Account intermittently throughout the year. So you're not looking for high-yield interest rates. In fact, probably the best place for these leftovers is in two regular passbook accounts.

Having a passbook savings account may be reminiscent of the way you saved money back in the days when you had a paper route or a baby-sitting business, but there's a lot to be said for the old system. You don't want to turn your PYP or Gift Account into instant money. That's the whole point. You want accounts that you add to steadily, week by week, that will eventually reward you. There's something fundamentally, organically satisfying about watching a bank account balance get a little bit bigger every week. So, the most important rule in managing these short-term accounts is: Don't get fancy!

3. Like the PYP Account, the Big Plans Account should be separate from your current checking account, but also separate from your short-term PYP Account and Gift Account. Having yet another separate account may seem unnecessary from a rational point of view, but we're not dealing with entirely rational behavior here. The reason to have a BP Account is the same reason that kings have countinghouses—to watch the money pile up. Whatever you're planning for, you want to see the money accumulating in the bank.

Keep your regular PYP Account running smoothly—continue to make your deposits every week.

Add steadily to your Gift Account.

But when you get some kind of bonanza, put it in the BP Account. That bonanza might be the birthday check from your godfather, the money you make from selling your dust-covered guitar, the $100 that your brother Fred finally paid back—or it could be extra commissions and bonuses.

Now, maybe your BP Account stays at the near-empty level for a while. But just having it set up is a motivator. In the past, perhaps, your bonanzas disappeared into the great mishmash of overdue bill payments, or got swallowed up in weekly expenses, or went into your current checking account. But if you have a BP Account, your bonanza money can go directly toward your future plans.

If you are single, the BP Account might go directly toward something that you've always wanted for yourself. If you are married, it's essential for you and your partner to discuss how this account is going to be used.

The BP Account represents a long-term goal, and reaching that goal should provide a meaningful reward for both of you. If it turns out that each of you has different "priority concerns," you and your partner could agree to have separate BP accounts.

Keeping separate accounts can be mutually beneficial. For example, your BP Account might be for an education fund; your spouse's, for home improvements. With your fund your kids will have a better chance of meeting college expenses; with your spouse's you'll be adding to the value of your home. In the long run the whole family is benefiting from both accounts, even though they're separate.

THE SPENDING

1. When you've reached your goal amount in your PYP Account—within three months if you've planned well—you simply take out the funds and *have* that splendid meal at a four-star restaurant. Then set a new PYP goal.

2. If gift giving means, to your psyche, another form of unleashed spending, then the Gift Account is extremely useful as a disciplinarian. During holiday times like December, when money tends to spill out in gobs and dollops, limit your spending to exactly what's in the Gift Account.

If you have 18 relatives to buy for, just divide the Gift Account balance by 18, and that's how much you can spend on Uncle Seth. Of course you can spend less on Uncle Seth and more on Uncle Merv—favoritism is up to you—but the bottom line doesn't change.

3. If your BP Account is for a special vacation, eventually you *might* have enough for that week in Cancun, and you'll find it was worth waiting for. This time you won't return from your vacation with that sinking feeling that you're going to have to face another credit card payment that you can't make.

On the other hand, if your BP Account is for a more serious expense—funds for your own or your children's education or a down payment on a house—you'll have the gratification of seeing that fund grow steadily. With the Big Plans Account you're not just dreaming about the future—you're planning for it.

You Don't Need Wizards

Of course there may be a friend or financial wizard who questions your wisdom in keeping funds in low-interest-bearing accounts.

"Look," that person may say, "you've got a credit card balance that's costing you 19.8 percent a month—and here you are trying to put away a few dollars in separate accounts that are giving you less than 7 percent. Why don't you use your combined savings to pay off some of that credit card debt? After all, it's the cost-effective thing to do!"

All true—mathematically, statistically, financially. But all those arguments neglect *your* needs. If you have stopped using your credit cards (step 2) and you've gone on a cash payment plan (step 3), your lines of credit will be taken care of in good order. Meanwhile you need these separate accounts to keep your financial house in order.

(Since your BP Account is a long-term savings, how-

KIDS AND COLLEGE—GETTING THERE FROM HERE

Almost any parent will automatically turn the Big Plans Account into an Awesome Tuition Account. Soaring tuition is an all-too-real reality, but if you are currently or prospectively a parent, there are three important things to remember:

1. If you start to save something *soon,* each month, in an interest-bearing account, you're in better shape than if you wait until later. With an illustration that is louder than a million words, here is a chart that compares the "early saver" and the "late saver" at the end of a 20-year period:

	EARLY SAVER	LATE SAVER
	Depositing $1,000 a year (about $83 a month) at 8%	Depositing nothing
Year 1	$ 1,083	0
Year 5	6,397	0
Year 10	15,939	0
	Depositing nothing, but building at 8%	Depositing $1,000 a year at 8%
Year 11	17,267	1,083
Year 20	35,471	15,939

In other words, if you started today and stopped saving after the 10th year, you would still have more than twice the amount of someone who *started* 10 years from now. And if you continued to save $1,000 a year from the 11th through the 20th years, you would have $53,939—as compared to the "late saver's" $15,939.

2. Your children are likely to become more resourceful if you keep them informed. When they get into their teen years, you might as well discuss awesome tuition with them—since they're certainly going to play a role in getting themselves through college. Let them know what your plans are and what they can do and talk about some reasonable expectations for their education.

3. The best you can do is the best you can do! If you have already come this far in the six-step action plan, you have proven that you have the resourcefulness to get through tough financial times. Ultimately that resourcefulness—combined with the fresh energy and ingenuity of your children—will help all of you manage the awesome tuition problem.

ever, you do want to get the highest investment returns on this account. That's something to consider as you "master your riches." See step 6.)

Raising Your Sights

When you have successfully completed steps 1 through 5, you have mastered all the tools for running a small but crucially important business—your own personal finances. In fact, when it's set up according to the action plan guidelines, that "business" may now run itself with a lot less thought and worry than you devoted to it before. That gives you more freedom to increase your earnings, make investment plans, and discover new opportunities. In other words your "business" will soon show a profit—and you can begin to think of creative ways to increase your income and begin making investments.

You're ready for the final step of the action plan.

S T E P 5 R E V I E W

1. With the "Leftovers" from step 3, set up a Plan Your Pleasures Account and a Gift Account and contribute to both weekly.

2. When you get any kind of "bonanza," use this money to start a Big Plans Account. Contribute to it whenever you can.

3. Within three months, spend your PYP funds on the reward decided on.

4. At gift-giving times, spend *only* what you have in your Gift Account.

5. Keep adding to your BP Account until you reach your goal.

6. Keep adding to these accounts after you make any withdrawals.

You're equipped to provide for your future pleasures and anticipated needs without relying on credit, and you're on your way to mastering your riches.

MASTER YOUR RICHES

· · · · · · · · · · · · · · · · · · · ·

As you gain increased control over your money, you'll become aware that some very positive transformations are taking place in your life. Any or all of the following are likely to occur:

- Because you are freed of worry from debt, you find that you become more confident in your decision making.
- Because you can see where the money is going, and you can control the way it's spent, you find that planning for the future is easier and more gratifying.
- Because your rewards increase (through your PYP and BP Accounts), every time you have additional income you begin to think more creatively about ways to increase your prosperity.

- Because you have experience in negotiating with creditors, you are better able to understand and deal with people in financial institutions. That's because you're dealing with *people* rather than with monolithic institutions that communicate via computer.

So, by taking the first five action steps you have already laid the foundation for the sixth step—mastering your riches.

The power you now control is money. Not just the cash in your hand or the cash in the bank but money in all its forms, including your own creditworthiness and your own earning power. That's where your riches are. You have the power not only to meet your payments but also to increase your income.

To do that, start with the following self-evaluation.

Evaluate Your Earning Power and Investment Savvy

There are many sound investments, but the soundest of all is yourself. If you build your own skills, rely on your abilities, increase your range, and get help when you need it, *you* are the investment that will succeed above all others. So, to begin mastering your riches, answer the following questions.

1. Assuming that you succeed in your current job, will you eventually make the kind of money you want?

If your answer is **yes** . . .

The next step toward mastering your riches is quite simple. You need to concentrate on succeeding in your job. If you think there are people who can help you succeed, consult with them. If you need additional training or you would benefit from courses, now is the time to investigate them. Explore every avenue to achieving the kind of success that you want to achieve—that's a direct line to achieving the wealth that you desire.

If your answer is **no** . . .

The journey ahead of you is a little more complicated, but it may be just as interesting and pleasurable. If your current job is *not* going to lead you toward the kind of wealth you want, it may be time to consider a career shift, look into educational opportunities that might lead to better-paying jobs, or look for other career opportunities within the organization you work for.

If your answer to question 1 was no, pay special attention to question 2.

2. Do you have a skill, talent, or ability that could be a source of extra income?

If your answer is **yes** . . .

The step toward mastering your riches is to tap that source of income. Here are just a few examples:

• Holding your current job, you might also have time to do a small amount of free-lance work. Although the income might not be great, you'll find that the extra work seems eminently worthwhile if that income is going into your BP Account.

• If you have skill in almost any trade or profession, there may be part-time teaching or consulting opportunities that you can explore.

• A hobby, an avocation, or work that you've been doing on a volunteer basis could produce income for you.

• You might start a part-time business from your home.

If your answer is **no** . . .

This could be the perfect time to begin building your skills in different areas. If you think further education or training would open some doors for you, get in touch with schools or institutions that offer courses and ask for catalogs.

Another method: During your next 10 conversations with friends or relatives, make a point of mentioning that you are looking for some ways to earn some extra income. Do they have any suggestions? Can they recommend other people who can help you?

Make a list of possible opportunities and see which ones seem the most attractive. If you can't make up your mind on which opportunity to pursue, there's a simple rule of thumb: *Choose one and do something about it.* You never know when one opportunity may lead to another. Often the biggest problem is just getting started.

3. If you had money to invest, would you know where to invest it?

If your answer is **yes** . . .

All you need is the money to invest. But where do you find that money if you don't have it right now?

One possibility is to put your BP Account to work in your investments to increase the earnings in that account. Of course you need to weigh carefully how high a risk you want to take when you are investing your BP Account. That's why it's essential for you to know something about risk/earnings ratios in investments. So . . .

If your answer is **no** . . .

It's important for you to learn something about this subject, either for immediate use or for the future. And if you feel inexperienced with investments and financial planning, here are some avenues to consider:

Take a class or two in financial planning and/or investments. Many night courses are designed expressly for people who have full-time jobs. They give you an introduction to various kinds of money instruments, tax considerations, and investment opportunities. You might not be in a position to use this information right away—but the class will give you an overall picture of what you can accomplish with money.

Often these courses are taught by investment counselors who want your business. So don't expect objective reporting when they're talking about investment opportunities. Learn what you can, try some other courses, and get a sampling of viewpoints before you lay out any money based on an instructor's recommendations.

Talk about money! This may sound elementary, but the fact is, when we're in debt any conversation about money, investments, or finances sends a shiver up the spine. We avoid it!

That will change as you get out of debt. Furthermore, you'll probably meet some people who enjoy making money, and you may discover that they're quite willing to talk about their experiences.

You're not necessarily looking for advice. Everyone's financial needs and priorities are different, so be wary of the person who knows "what you should do." But you definitely need information from all sources—the more, the better. (For some informed, readable, and occasionally entertaining investment books, see Appendix E.)

As you may have noticed, all these suggestions concerning income and investment knowledge focus on fairly predictable, ordinary procedures for earning money. There's no flashy advice here for buying an 89-unit condominium with nothing down or swapping your junk bonds for High-Top J-Test Q-Factored Money Interest Overbearing Backfire Zoom-Return Flash Funds.

There's a reason why mastering your riches takes more tried-and-true earning rather than flash-and-dash money manipulation. If you've been losing sleep because of your debts, you know that high-flying expectations are usually accompanied by a low-level bomber squad of anxieties. The goal of the action plan is to *reduce* your anxieties while helping you control your money so you can get what you want.

Focus on Your Goals

As you gain greater confidence in your ability to manage money and make investments, you'll get lots of advice, assistance, and insight from numerous sources. Keeping an open mind is, of course, an asset. But looking to yourself—again, your soundest investment—is always your best bet. Your investment decisions are likely to be much clearer if you know *why* you make each investment, *what* your goals are, and then use appropriate strategies to achieve those goals.

If you are still struggling to meet your monthly payments, and future wealth seems very far away, then the most important step may be the one that you're about to take right now:

1. Write down what your goals are! You might not be able to express these goals in terms of dollars and cents right now. More likely your goals may seem like distant wish fulfillment. But it's important to put them in some concrete form. Putting them in writing is, for now, concrete enough.

Among the questions to answer when you consider your goals:

• Are you content with your current living arrangement, or do you want a different kind of home in a different place? For instance, if you're living in a mid-city apartment, your goal may be a farmhouse in a field alongside a babbling brook. (For someone else, on the other hand, that might be the soul of a rural nightmare.) For now, never mind whether that goal is realistic. Just write it down.

• Are there places you eagerly want to travel to? If so, where? Do you envision a long trip or short escapes? Lavish living or simple retreats?

• What are your professional goals? Where do you see yourself 10 years from now? What would be the ideal position for you?

• What are other activities and avocations that you

■ **INVESTMENT CAVEATS**

You might want to keep in mind a couple of truisms, no matter how you invest:

No Investment Is "Perfect"

Whether you're starting your own business, buying real estate, or investing in Hydro-Gyro Model Airplanes, you can be sure that there's a more profitable business or a better deal "just around the corner." Well, keep an eye on what's going on around the corner, but concentrate on watching the investment you've made. If your investment doesn't seem to be working out—and some of them don't!—consider it a trial run.

None of us enjoys it when the upside isn't as spectacular as we'd dreamed. But even when it looks as if someone's making bigger money in more exotic ways, focus on your own plan. Find out what others are doing right and what they're doing wrong; then make your own investments in your own way.

If You Come Closer to Your Goal, You've Made a Successful Investment

For instance, if you invest in a piece of property because you want it for retirement, then you don't care whether the land value of that property doubles or halves in the next decade. You weren't in it for the short-term cash; what you wanted was exactly what you got—a property for retirement. And that's very satisfying.

Should your goals change? *Will* they change? Of course! Goal setting and prioritizing are not one-time tasks but ongoing exercises in the process of mastering your riches.

would like to pursue further? How involved would you like to be in these activities 10 years from now? Twenty years?

• If you have children, what are your goals for them? Ideally, where would you like them to go to college? How about graduate schools? And if they have a special talent or ability (gymnastics? figure skating? violin?), what kind of special instruction opportunities would you like them to have?

If you are married or living with someone, have your partner write about his or her goals separately. Don't consult with each other while you're doing your lists. But do talk about them afterward.

Even if those goals are pie-in-the-sky right now, just recognizing what you want—and what your partner wants—can be very illuminating.

2. Immediately after you've made up this list, go back through it and number your priorities. For example, if your list of goals includes earning an advanced management degree, buying a farmhouse in the country, getting promoted to a high-powered job, taking a two-week retreat in Nepal, and joining a golf club, obviously you have some serious choices to make.

You don't have to make those choices right now. But it's important to list your priorities. For a single person the order might go something like this:

1. Advanced management degree
2. Two weeks in Nepal
3. Golf club membership
4. Vice presidency at Superglaze
5. Farmhouse in the country

If you foresee starting a family soon, or you already have children, your priorities probably take on a much different order. You might relish the two-week retreat in Nepal, and a farmhouse in the country is certainly desirable, but will those things really come before child care, music lessons, and college savings? For the married person with children, the priority list would be more likely to look like this:

1. Advanced management degree
2. Vice presidency at Superglaze
3. Start the kids' college fund
4. Golf club membership
5. Farmhouse in the country
6. Two months in Nepal

Now, each one of these goals carries a price tag. The trouble is, if you try to get all these things at once—and work frenetically toward having them all—there's a real chance that you won't quite get any of them.

On the other hand, if you can prioritize your list, all you have to concern yourself with is achieving the first thing on your list.

The best way to begin mastering your riches is to know what you need those riches for—what you're going to use them for. All of your goals may be achievable. But how you set priorities will probably determine whether you achieve them.

Financial Peace of Mind

J. Paul Getty, of oil wealth fame, had a personal formula for success that came in three parts:

1. Rise early.
2. Work hard.
3. Strike oil!

Our formula for financial peace of mind is like his but with some important revisions:

1. Rise early if you have to.
2. By all means work hard.
3. *And don't count on striking oil!*

If you follow Getty's advice, you might end up like J. Paul Getty. (Who needs it?) Or you might spend your whole life *wishing* you were J. Paul Getty. (You definitely don't need that.)

But if you follow the steps for financial peace of mind, you might end up smart, successful . . . and free from financial worry. With all that going for you, why bother with oil wells?

STEP 6 REVIEW

1. Evaluate your earning power at your current job. If it falls short of your future needs/wants, consider different or supplemental career opportunities as well as educational opportunities.

2. Evaluate your investment knowledge. If it's insufficient, take classes, read, and talk to people about their financial experiences.

3. List your goals for the future. Consider such factors as location and type of home, places to visit, activities to get involved in, and professional achievements to make.

4. Prioritize your goals.

5. Aim for one goal at a time.

You've been empowered by taking action and regaining control of your money matters. Now it's time to get on with your life!

EMPOWERMENT THROUGH THE SIX STEPS

When you complete the sixth step of the action plan, you should take a moment to reward yourself. Look at what you've accomplished—and how far you've come. You have ample evidence that you *can* take control over your money:

Step 1

By drawing a financial profile of yourself, you faced facts. You discovered that you could account for where the money was going—and reduce your spending in certain areas.

Step 2

You locked up your credit cards. You proved that you don't need them to get by, and you don't need the rush you get from being able to use your plastic any time and anywhere.

Step 3

By going on the lump-sum budget plan, you discovered that you can pay as you go. You don't have to rely on credit. In all likelihood you also discovered that you probably don't miss the things you have to "do without"—especially when the trade-off is greater peace of mind.

Step 4

If you had to make new arrangements with your creditors, you honed your ability to deal with financial institutions. Better yet, you discovered that you don't have to run away from your obligations. You are able to meet your debts on reliable terms—and you even have some power to determine those terms.

Step 5

In this step you set up three accounts that help you work toward obtaining future rewards. Now you don't have to *wish* for your ship to come in—it's already on its way.

Step 6

As you begin to master your riches, you *use* the power that you've learned to control. Now you can learn more about money, set your goals, and establish priorities. You begin to have more say in your financial future than you ever had before.

By following the six steps of the action plan, you have put yourself on a program that can help you reduce your debt, meet your daily needs, and prepare for the future.

The process of empowerment begins from the first day. You *can* make bets on your future, as long as you're not betting *everything*. With the six-step plan you have more control over your earning power as well as your spending power. Above all, the plan gives you room to enjoy what you already have—and therefore the power to enjoy life more.

II

SPECIAL
TACTICS FOR
TOUGH
TIMES

TACTIC 1 ......

DEALING WITH COLLECTION AGENCIES

....

If you have to negotiate with collection agents, there's one thing you will probably notice right away: They've had lots of practice at this, and you haven't.

Let's say you have received a letter from the collection agent. It may be very legal-looking, and it may threaten *action* (probably without specifying what action) unless you pay your bill within 48 hours. Let's further suppose that you can't pay your bill right away, so you don't. And a few days later you receive a phone call from a collection agent.

Does that agent have the right to call?

Yes. But the 1978 Fair Debt Collection Practices Act dictates exactly what collection agents may and may not do.

■ **WHAT COLLECTION AGENTS CAN'T DO**

- They can't call you at inconvenient hours—that is, before eight in the morning or after nine at night.
- They can't call friends and relatives, except to ask for your address or telephone number. (And even that isn't allowed if they can find this information elsewhere.)
- They can't call your place of work if they can reach you at home. (And they can't call you at work *under any circumstances* if you, or your employer, inform the agent in writing that you don't wish to be contacted at your place of business.)
- They can't make *harassing* calls—which usually means they can't call more than once a week.
- They can't pretend to be someone they're not—your uncle Hal, a cop, a sheriff, or a lawyer.
- They can't speak directly to you if you notify the collection agency that you are represented by an attorney; they have to contact your attorney.
- They can't gang up on you: only one agent from the agency can call you. If a number of agents are calling—or if the same agent uses different pseudonyms—the actions of that agency are illegal. (The one agent who contacts you, however, is allowed to use a single pseudonym.)
- They can't distribute any information that could harm your reputation in your business or community. (Hence no one can list your name in the paper as a debtor.) If an agent tells you that your professional reputation will be ruined by nonpayment of debt, you can threaten legal action.
- They can't threaten to take away your car, foreclose on your house, or seize your personal property. An agent may suggest that legal action can lead to such things, but any such action needs to be brought separately. And he's completely out of line if he threatens you with arrest or imprisonment.
- They can't make anonymous, annoying, or repetitive phone calls.
- They cannot "disturb the peace" or threaten violent action when they visit your home (which they are allowed to do). And they can't visit more than once during a 30-day

period, except for reasonable follow-up visits. (Because visitations are often impractical as well as inconvenient, you'll probably be called rather than visited.)

- They can't make false statements about the status of the debt or falsely suggest dire consequences if you don't pay it.
- They can't collect an additional fee that is not authorized under the terms of the debt agreement.
- They can't demand or accept any checks that are dated more than five days ahead, except under very specific written conditions.
- They can't charge you with collect calls or telegram fees.
- And they can't communicate by postcard.

Collection agents rarely use out-and-out intimidation anymore. The 1978 Fair Debt Collection Practices Act put an end to most of that. You don't need to worry about a thug coming to your door or some impostor in a sheriff's uniform appearing to seize your television, refrigerator, and stereo. In fact most collection agents are masterful at controlling their language and their tempers.

Nonetheless the good ones are very good at what they do—which is making people pay up. What they have to work with is the guilt and shame that many people feel when they're in debt.

If you suggest repaying a small amount, your proposal is likely to be met with thinly veiled scorn. If you say you simply can't pay, the agent will imply that you're making a huge mistake. And if you don't respond at all, the collection agent may threaten legal action.

So, what *do* you do at this point?

Know the Score

First, know what you're up against. If you know your rights and the collection agency tactics you're likely to

■
WHAT COLLECTION AGENTS MUST DO

- They must identify themselves and the company they work for.
- They have to tell you why they're calling—which account they're trying to collect and the amount they claim you owe your creditor.
- Within five days after the call, they have to send you a letter that specifies the same data—the name of the collection agency, name of the creditor, and the amount you owe. (The letter will usually state the amount, which is assumed to be valid unless you dispute it within 30 days.)

encounter, you can avoid a lot of anguish and get on with resolving this problem.

PROTECTING YOURSELF

If an agent violates any of the rules concerning collections or if you believe you are being harassed, contact your state Bureau of Consumer Protection. The bureau will send you a complaint form. Fill out and send in the form along with a copy of correspondence from the collection agency, canceled checks, contracts, or any other materials that substantiate your complaint. On the complaint form you should identify the agent who has been contacting you or the person at the collection agency who is aware of your complaint.

The bureau will investigate your complaint, and if necessary, a mediator will be assigned to handle your request. While the mediator will attempt to resolve the issue, he or she cannot act as your attorney. The bureau can go to court only in the name of the state when it has been shown that a company has violated specific provisions of the Unfair Trade Practices and Consumer Protection Law.

Keep in mind that the collection agency represents the

creditor, and the creditor is legally liable for any actions of the agent. While the agent may try anything that's legally feasible to collect on the account, the agency has a disincentive for going too far. If the creditor consistently gets consumer complaints about its collection agency, it may decide to change. And that's a *real* loss for the collection agency.

VERIFYING THE CLAIM

If you think an unfair or inaccurate claim has been made against you, write a letter to the collection agency stating that you dispute the claim. Mention that, under Section 809 (b) of the federal Fair Debt Collection Practices Act, the agency must provide you with verification of the debt and is prohibited from taking any further action until the verification is provided.

You have 30 days to dispute the claim.

WITHSTANDING INTIMIDATION

Given all the requirements and limitations imposed on them, why is it that collection agents can be so convincing and, in some instances, subtly intimidating?

First of all, if you truly want to pay your debts and you haven't been able to, you already feel guilty about the overdue bill. The agent knows that, and he'll do whatever he can to make you feel even *more* guilty.

Second, the agent usually has ways to suggest that someone more powerful may take your account in hand if you refuse to pay. How to imply this without being threatening (and thereby violating the law) takes some ingenuity, but there are ways:

- The agent may say that "they" won't be happy with the repayment plan you're proposing. (Who are "*they*"? What can "they" do about it?)

- He may also suggest that your account will be "moved higher up in the collection cycle." (The fact is, apart from legal action there is no "higher cycle.")
- Or the agent may say that your account will be referred to "someone at the next level." (Actually the agent doesn't want his supervisor to deal with your account at all, because that would be an admission that the agent can't handle it himself.)

Although such phrases are for the most part meaningless, they do manage to suggest that something more ominous and dreadful will occur if you don't comply.

The threat of legal action may be real, but such action has to be brought by the creditor rather than the collection agency. And keep in mind that legal action is an expensive recourse for the creditor. It's unlikely that the action will be worth taking unless your outstanding account balance is very large. After all, the creditor went to the collection agency precisely to avoid action. And the agent would rather settle with you than go to the next step.

Resolve the Problem: Turn the Tables

If you have already decided you want to work out a repayment plan, why not make the call yourself? After the first call or letter from the collection agent, inform him that you're working out a repayment plan and you'll call him in five days with a proposal.

Five days later, get in touch with the agent and outline your plan.

He may argue that the payments you propose are not big enough: "they" won't accept your proposal.

Your reply?

"I've completely reviewed my financial situation, and the amount I've proposed is what I can do to meet my obligations. I'll be sending you a check for $ _____ on

Monday, along with a letter to confirm the plan I've just proposed. I'll call you on Friday to make sure you've gotten it. Please don't call at home or at my office. I know this plan will work, and I intend to stay up to date with the monthly payments I propose."

The agent may tell you it's not enough.

- *Tell him it's the best you can do.*

His language may become stronger.

- *Tell him you may have to file a complaint with his supervisor.*

He may tell you that the creditor won't accept your repayment plan.

- *Tell him this is the only way you can meet all your obligations.*

The agent may threaten legal action.

- *Tell him that's entirely unnecessary, insofar as you've just described a very reasonable repayment plan.*

Keep in mind that despite how he sounds, it's in the agent's best interest to have you repay: the number of collections he makes determines his promotions and raises.

CONFIRM IN WRITING

Then write the letter confirming your repayment plan and requesting no more phone calls.

The letter doesn't need to be written in legalese. Simple English will suffice. Here's a sample:

DATE

Name of Agent
Name of Collection Agency
Address

Dear (Name of Agent):

Regarding Account #8064329383 with Carry-On Credit
Card Company, this is to confirm the repayment plan
that I proposed during our conversation of May 1, 19___.

As I specified at that time, I am enclosing my first
payment of $_____, which leaves a balance of $_____.
I intend to pay the balance in monthly installments of
$_____, which I will send to your attention on the ___th
day of every month.

It is my understanding that no legal action will be
brought against me as long as I continue to make timely
payments in fulfillment of this debt.

Please take note of my request that I receive no further
phone calls at my home or place of business.

Thank you for your attention to this matter.

                              Yours truly,

    The check that you enclose—and all future checks—
should be made out to the collection agency, with the name
of your creditor and the account number also on the check.
(If you make it out to the creditor, that company will have

to pass it along to the collection agency, since the agency is now handling your account.)

HAVING YOUR TERMS ACCEPTED

If the agency, after receiving this, actually wishes to dispute the amount of payment, the collection agent is entitled to make one more phone call to let you know the consequences of your request that you not be contacted further. You then have the option of renegotiating if you want to.

In all likelihood the agent will simply send you an agency form for your signature. Read it carefully to make sure it confirms the terms set forth in your own letter without setting any further conditions. If the agency sends you a legal-looking form that contains obscure language— or if you question anything that's stated in the form— return it with a query rather than sign it.

Whether or not you eventually sign the agency's form, as long as you continue to make timely payments it is unlikely that the collection agent will continue to pursue your account. However, if you don't sign the form, you might be notified of legal action, in which case you will need an attorney.

2

NEGOTIATING WITH THE IRS ... AND OTHER TAX AUTHORITIES

If you owe back taxes that you can't pay, negotiating with the IRS should be number one on your list of priorities. Uncle Sam is vigilant when it comes to collecting his taxes. If you have underreported your taxes and a judgment is entered against you, the government can garnishee your wages, place a lien on your property, put a levy on your bank account, or freeze your assets.

The IRS can also repossess your car, house, or other property and sell them at auction. And if you are regarded as a tax evader, the IRS may attempt to bring criminal proceedings against you. In other words the IRS has many ways of making life miserable for you.

Dealing with Uncle Sam

The best thing to do if you owe back taxes is to negotiate with the IRS as you would with any other creditor. If you owe a lump sum that you simply can't pay, the IRS will usually allow you to work out a repayment plan. However, while other creditors might settle for less than the full amount, the IRS will always demand full repayment.

If your tax situation involves more than working out a repayment agreement, then you should look for an attorney who is experienced in taxes (see "Resource 3: Attorneys").

The IRS charges interest, and it can also set penalties on the unpaid balance. But you may be able to avoid further penalties by communicating directly with your local Internal Revenue office.

In any case, it's important to get back taxes out of the way. Unlike a bad credit report or a bankruptcy that disappears from your record after a number of years, a charge to the government can pursue you for the rest of your life.

Federal income taxes are not dischargeable in the case of either a business or personal bankruptcy (see "Tactic 8: Bankruptcy"). When an individual or a business files for bankruptcy, there's an automatic stay that prevents the IRS from filing liens or levies or freezing assets. So you're protected for a limited period of time. But the outstanding debt to the IRS will eventually have to be repaid.

A frequent problem that small businesses encounter is in not paying their withholding or social security taxes. If you are self-employed or paying yourself a salary out of a small business—whether it's a corporation, an S corporation, or a partnership—be sure to keep your payments to the IRS up to date. It's much easier to recover from a business failure and begin anew if you have taken care of your tax payments.

Other Taxes

If you owe back taxes to the county, state, or city, these governments also have the right to take a number of legal actions against you. Like the IRS, they can garnishee your wages, collect against your property, levy your bank account, or put a lien on your property.

Of course you don't want any of these things to happen—and there's no reason why they should, unless you try to evade calls and notices. In all cases there are certain procedures for disputing or appealing the claim, and the governing authority is obliged to let you know what these procedures are. So if you get a notice in the mail that you owe more taxes, the first thing you should do is review your filing. If you conclude that your figures were correct in the first place, write back immediately and let them know that you wish to appeal the decision. After that the procedures that are followed will depend on the tax authority you're dealing with.

What if you owe an amount that's more than you can pay? Just as you would with a credit card company, call or write to the taxing authority and suggest a repayment plan. Even if you are able to pay only $20 a month, call and suggest a monthly repayment plan.

Of course, if the taxing authority threatens criminal action or liens, you will need the immediate advice of legal counsel.

TACTIC 3 ······

NEGOTIATING WITH UTILITY COMPANIES

■ ■

Most of us assume that in addition to having constitutional rights to a TV and telephone, we also have the right to heat, light, and running water. Usually we can't "cut back" drastically on such necessities, even in times of indebtedness. If we're behind in our utility bills, our goal is to negotiate for terms that we can meet or else take action to make sure none of these services are cut off.

You are likely to receive numerous notices before any utility company will terminate service. In some states, even if the utility company has sent many warnings, it must also send a termination notice at least 10 days before a cutoff. In addition, most states have a ruling that a utility company representative must visit you *in person* several days before the termination date. (If you're not home or you don't come to the door, the visitor can leave a notice rather than speaking to you directly.) In most states the utility cannot turn off your gas or power immediately before a weekend or a legal holiday.

As in every situation where your payment is overdue, the most important step is to get in touch with a representative of the utility company and let that person know what you intend to do. The service representative who answers your call will probably be satisfied if you agree to "go current" on your bill.

One thing to remember is that the utility company usually has a strong disincentive for bringing any legal action against you. In most states any legal action ends up involving the public utilities commission, which translates into extensive red tape and expense for the company.

One on one with the utility company representative, you can negotiate terms in a number of different ways. As usual, be honest about your financial situation and emphasize your intent to pay. You can propose several kinds of repayment plans. For instance:

1. "I am currently reviewing my financial statement. I will pay my current balance this month. I propose to pay off the balance during the next _____ months."

2. "I can't pay anything right now because. . . ." (Explain!) "However, I will be able to pay next month's bill in full. In addition, I will send X percent of the outstanding balance. After that I will pay off the rest of the balance in _____ equal monthly installments."

3. "I'm sending in my bill today with payment on the current balance and $20 on the outstanding balance. I intend to keep current from now on, and I will continue to pay as much as I can on the outstanding balance."

The utility company representative may propose other terms. If the bill is large, the representative may want to refer you to someone else in the company. Whichever way the negotiations lead, ask for assurance that your call has been noted on the computer.

Whether or not you have to continue your negotiations

with someone higher up, immediately send a letter outlining the proposal you made during your initial phone conversation. A suggested letter:

May 5, 19__

Howth Hill Utilities
231 Riverrun Road
Finnigan, WA
RE: Account # 09879876

Dear Service Representative:

This is to confirm the proposal I made to you in our conversation today. I intend to pay the overdue balance on the above account in monthly installments of $20 and to keep current with my bill.

Enclosed find payment of $54.97. This amount includes payment of $34.97 for this month, plus payment of $20 on the overdue balance.

It is my understanding that my service will be continued under this agreement.

Sincerely yours,

If You Have to Appeal . . .

If a utility company continues to threaten you with a cutoff of service, immediately contact your state public utility commission's Department of Consumer Services.

The PUC is usually included in your state government listings in the phone book.

When you contact the PUC, describe your negotiations with the utility company. If you have had correspondence with the company, the PUC representative may ask for documentation.

If you have a complaint against the company, you may request an "informal" hearing. This usually can be done by phone. You also are allowed a "formal complaint" to the whole public utility commission if the first hearing is decided against you.

If your service is discontinued in spite of your efforts, and the commission subsequently intervenes in your behalf, your service has to be turned on soon—usually within three working days.

The details of PUC policies differ from state to state. But in all states the commissions are set up to protect the consumer. So don't hesitate to contact the PUC if you have any kind of difficulty negotiating with a utility company.

If You Need Financial Assistance . . .

If you simply can't meet payments in time to forestall a cutoff of services, you might turn to one of the many energy assistance programs that have been set up throughout the United States. Check the state listings or "human services" listings in the "blue pages" section of your phone book.

In many states the energy assistance offices provide funding to help pay for all kinds of heating costs, including oil, coal, gas, kerosene, and wood. Because many furnaces require electricity to keep operating, the energy assistance funds may also cover the cost of electricity.

Negotiating with Your Long-Distance Telephone Service

If the long-distance telephone company notifies you that your service is about to be cut off, contact a company representative immediately. In general, it's far easier to prevent telephone service from being cut off than it is to have it restored once it *is* cut off. Usually partial payment of a bill is sufficient to maintain telephone service, as long as that payment is accompanied by an explanation and a promise to pay the balance in installments.

If you receive a warning notice, call the 800 number shown on a recent bill. The points to make are:

- You intend to pay the bill in full.
- Because of the size of the bill, you are restricting your personal use of long-distance service until the bill is paid off.
- You are putting a check in the mail today for partial payment.

It's likely that you can make all these arrangements with the first person you talk to at the telephone company. If you send a partial-payment check immediately, you will probably continue to receive notices in the mail. In most circumstances service will be continued as long as you aren't running up excessive new long-distance charges.

Of course when you send in your payment you also need to write a brief letter reiterating the proposal you made in your phone conversation.

When you run up a bill with one long-distance service, you may be sorely tempted to switch to another. A word of advice here: If you're thinking of changing, get the first bill paid off first. Your bill is overdue because you're making more long-distance calls than you can afford to make—not because you're spending a few pennies per minute too much. If you just change services without changing your long-distance phone habits, you may end up with double the bills to pay.

Local Telephone Service

Your local telephone service is one of the basic necessities of your life. If you've been tossing your local telephone bills in a drawer and you're now being threatened with a cutoff of service, take those threats very seriously.

Your local bill is probably fairly stable every month. When you call the company to discuss your overdue balance, let the service representative know that you intend to keep up with current charges. Then specify how much you intend to pay on the overdue amount every month. For example, if your overdue balance is $80 and your monthly bill is $25, you can suggest: "I'll keep current every month, and I'll pay an additional $10 for the next eight months." Then write a check for $35 and send it in with a letter repeating the substance of your conversation.

There may be interest charges on the outstanding balance, but it's unlikely that you'll have to speak to a higher-up in the company, as long as you maintain your payments.

This is also a great time to reduce the "extras" that you may have on your telephone service. For example, if you signed up for call forwarding and call waiting but you never use those features, you might as well discontinue them. They only cost extra.

TACTIC 4

NEGOTIATING WITH A LANDLORD

Suppose you are renting an apartment that costs $900 per month, and you fail to make payment on the date the payment is due. Whether or not you receive calls or reminders during the month, you are very likely to receive a "notice of default" before the end of the month. The notice tells you that you are 30 days overdue on the rent. It may also inform you that your next notice will be an eviction notice.

What recourse do you have?

1. Contact the landlord immediately and notify him or her of your intent to pay.

If the landlord refuses to speak to you or refers you to an attorney, then you will probably need your own lawyer to protect your rights as a tenant.

However, if the landlord agrees to give you more time . . .

• Propose a settlement on the rent that's in arrears. You might arrange to pay the rent you owe in monthly installments rather than a lump sum. For instance, if your rent is $900 per month, you might agree to pay an additional $100 per month for the next nine months ($1,000 per month in rent).

• Whatever arrangement the landlord agrees to verbally, put it in writing. For example:

"To confirm our verbal agreement of July 21, 1991, I acknowledge that I am in default of one month's rent ($900). To cure the default I agree to pay $1,000 per month on the first of each month for the next nine months. After _____ (date), I will resume payments of $900 per month. No other terms of the lease are affected by this agreement."

If the landlord *doesn't* agree to give you more time . . .

• Under the terms of most leases the landlord can serve an eviction notice. The landlord also may enter the apartment, remove your possessions, and change the locks.

• In this case you will probably need a lawyer as soon as possible to avoid eviction. Your goal is to take your case before the landlord-tenant court. (Once the case is in court, it's much more difficult for the landlord to throw you out of your apartment.)

Of course, if you hire an attorney, you will have to pay an attorney's fees. But this step is urgent and unavoidable if you want to continue residence.

(For more on finding a lawyer, see "Resource 3: Attorneys.")

• The attorney will tell you what rights you have as a tenant. (These rights differ in each state and city.) Your counsel will also help you file and plead your case in the landlord-tenant court. Having an attorney on your side almost invariably helps you gain time. The threat of a lengthy legal proceeding will often prevent a landlord from taking precipitate action.

WHAT TO DO IF YOU CAN'T MEET YOUR MORTGAGE PAYMENTS

• •

Just as credit card companies have reasons to negotiate, so do the holders of home mortgages. In the event that you fail to pay your mortgage, the lender is restricted to specific legal proceedings before foreclosing on your home or property. Keep in mind that foreclosure is really a last resort for the lender. Not only are the proceedings lengthy and expensive, but the mortgage holder may not recoup the full value of the mortgage. Since the number of foreclosures on homes increased 12-fold during the eighties, mortgage holders have been overburdened with foreclosures and wish to avoid them.

Your mortgage is governed by the mortgage document itself and by various state laws with respect to mortgages. A mortgage note typically contains a default clause that says if you fail to make a principal-and-interest payment on a certain day—and for 30 days thereafter—you will be in default under the note or mortgage.

In the event of default the lender has the right to declare the entire balance of the mortgage due and payable, but the lender is required to notify you of the default. Then you have a right to cure the default, immediately or at any time during the foreclosure proceedings, by making payment of the entire amount due.

How to Avoid Foreclosure Proceedings

If you are unable to pay your mortgage and you receive a default notice, it's imperative to take the following action.

1. Contact the mortgage holder—whether it's a bank or another lending institution—and ask for a meeting with an officer. Be clear and honest about your situation. If the earner in the family has recently been unemployed or disabled, let the lender know that. Or perhaps an illness in your family has made it difficult for you or your spouse to work. Do you have reason to believe the situation is temporary? Outline your prospects for the future.

The lender may suggest a way to refinance the loan. That could mean smaller monthly payments over a longer period of time, at higher interest rates.

2. If the lending institution is not willing to make a counteroffer to help you avoid foreclosure, contact the mortgage insurer. If there's a foreclosure, the insurer often has to pay between 20 and 25 percent of the original loan. So the insurer is better off if you can stay in the house, refinance your loan, and find a way to meet your monthly payments. Therefore, after talking with you, a representative of the insurer might be able to speak directly to the lender and recommend a schedule that will allow you to catch up with payments. In some instances the insurer and lender might provide help in the form of free financial counseling or partial-repayment plans.

The next-best alternative, from the insurer's point of view, is to help you sell your house before the bank forecloses. In fact that's an advantage for everyone: the lending institution doesn't get stuck with the property and court costs, the insurer doesn't have to pay as much to the lender, and you don't have a foreclosure listed in your credit history.

What to Do in the Event of Foreclosure

If you can't reach agreement on repayment terms and simply can't meet your payments, the mortgage holder may begin foreclosure proceedings. A foreclosure proceeding is a legal proceeding that requires the mortgage holder to file a complaint against you, alleging that you have defaulted on the mortgage.

1. As soon as you receive notice of a foreclosure action, seek legal counsel (see "Resource 3: Attorneys"). There are many ways that a lawyer can help you keep your house until you can meet the payments or sell it on your own.

2. When the mortgage holder files a complaint against you, you have a right as the borrower to come into court and defend yourself by filing an answer to the complaint. (Your lawyer will review with you the defenses that can be made in court.) Then you have a hearing on the question of whether or not you have defaulted on the mortgage.

3. If you lose in the hearing—if the court finds that you did not make the monthly payment as required—a judgment will be entered against you. Once the judgment has been entered, you can appeal to a higher court.

4. If you don't appeal, the lender can proceed with an action of foreclosure. The judgment will be given to a sheriff of the county through a writ of *praecipe,* and the sheriff will serve notice on you that a judgment has been entered. When the judgment has been docketed, the sheriff can begin formal foreclosure proceedings, which will require the sale of the property at a sheriff's sale.

The purpose of the sale is to let the lender recover the full amount owed on the principal—the remaining balance of the mortgage. When the house and property have been sold, the lender can use the proceeds to pay off the loan.

5. Before the sale occurs, you as homeowner in most cases *still* have the right to cure the default by paying the judgment. Paying the full amount you owe to the mortgage holder prior to the sheriff's sale will stop the sale.

6. Other ways to stop the sale include filing for bankruptcy and negotiating with the mortgage company. Often judgments can be renegotiated downward, or they can be opened again. Judgments can also be challenged with various arguments filed by an attorney in court.

CONSOLIDATING YOUR DEBT

Conceptually, debt consolidation is a neat-and-tidy way to bundle all your outstanding debt into one package that you pay off in timely installments. By taking out one big loan at a favorable interest rate, you have the cash to close down all your other credit card and charge card accounts. Then you just have one bill to pay every month, the principal-plus-interest on that single consolidated loan.

Of course there is no "automatic" way to get a single loan to consolidate your debts, but you might be able to obtain one through a bank or, if you are a member, from a credit union. Any lending institution has the right to check your credit report, and your request may be refused on the basis of your past record. (See "Tactic 7: Checking Your Credit Report.") However, as long as you have a steady income, you will probably be given a fair hearing. Your income level, rather than your credit record, may be the deciding factor.

Bank policies vary, and so do interest rates. If you are turned down for a loan at one bank, do not assume that all the others will also turn you down. On the other hand, if you are offered a loan by one bank, try several others to compare interest rates and terms.

A Caveat

You shouldn't even consider consolidating unless you're firmly committed to incurring no new debt. If you begin using your cards again, you'll owe not only a payment to the bank every month but also the minimum payments on the new credit card charges. You won't be able to keep up with both, so you'll have to borrow from somewhere else. A spiral of borrowing will begin, and you will go steadily deeper into debt. The end of this road? Bankruptcy.

The Pros and Cons

There are a number of excellent reasons to consider debt consolidation as a tactic:

- Besides the convenience, consolidating is psychologically rewarding. One check to make out every month, one loan to repay, and when you make the last payment on that loan, you're done!
- You can shop around for a more favorable interest rate than you get from credit card companies.
- Since you pay off the entire balance on all your credit cards, your credit record will not reflect any more overdue payments. (For more information on credit records, see "Tactic 7: Checking Your Credit Report.")

- If you use a home-equity line of credit, you get a tax advantage. The IRS no longer allows taxpayers to take a deduction for interest paid on revolving credit card accounts, but a homeowner can still deduct the interest paid on mortgage on a residence.

There are, however, also disadvantages:

- Too often, consolidating seems like a cure-all, and if you view it that way and give in to the temptation to open new accounts or unlock your credit cards, consolidating can be very risky indeed. If you take out a home-equity loan or home-equity line of credit to consolidate your debt, and you default on that loan, the bank or lending institution that holds the second mortgage can't automatically foreclose on your house, because the first mortgage holder also has first rights to the property. Still, defaulting on a home-equity loan can jeopardize the ownership of your home.
- You have to have that lump sum of cash to pay the consolidated loan payments on time every month. If you get paid once a week, that means you have to be sure not to spend that cash before the loan payment is due. Because individual credit and charge card payments are usually due on different dates, you might find it easier to pay smaller increments on different dates, as your cash comes in.

How to Consolidate

If you do decide to consolidate your debts, here's how to go about it:

1. Calculate how much money you need to pay off all your credit and charge accounts. Use the Credit Card and Charge Card Worksheet in Appendix A to find out how much you need to borrow.

2. Before you visit a bank or credit union to request a loan, figure out what you can afford to pay every month. Line C of the worksheet in Appendix C will give you this figure. Since this is the *absolute maximum* you can pay every month, you know you can't agree to repayment terms in excess of that amount.

3. If you are a homeowner, decide whether you want to take out a home-equity loan.

4. Shop around for terms and interest rates. If you're looking for a home-equity loan, the interest will usually be linked to the "prime" lending rate—the rate at which banks borrow money from other institutions. If the prime rate is 11 percent, for example, the bank will probably lend the money to you at a point or two above prime—that is, 12 or 13 percent. Your interest will go up when the prime rate goes up, but it will also go down when the prime rate goes down. (When did credit card interest ever go *down*?)

5. When you meet with an officer of the bank or lending institution, be sure to find out whether there are any charges for opening the account.

6. If you do sign up for the loan, mail payments immediately to all the accounts that you're paying off. Make sure you keep your credit cards locked up and take out no other loans until your debt consolidation loan is completely paid off.

T A C T I C **7** ● ● ● ● ● ●

CHECKING YOUR CREDIT REPORT

● ●

While you're getting your financial house in order, you should check your credit report to make sure the information about you is accurate. Your record can be reviewed by potential creditors. It can also be reviewed by a prospective employer if you are being considered for a job. So if there are inaccuracies in the record, they could come back to haunt you in the future—either when you're applying for a loan or when you're applying for a new job.

You can't change the plain facts that are listed in your credit history. On the other hand, you don't want misleading or inaccurate information on your record.

After you check your record, you can:

- Correct inaccuracies
- Include *favorable* information about paid-off loans, salary increases, new employment, or other relevant facts

- Take steps to have unverified information removed from the record
- Write brief statements about nonpayments or late payments that will be filed with your credit history (Those explanations must be sent by the credit bureau to anyone who inquires about your record.)

If you take these actions, you might be able to significantly improve your profile. And your statements can clarify the record—so no one will think you were intentionally delinquent or that you attempted to evade your creditors. Those changes could be deciding factors when you apply for a loan to buy a car or house or apply for a new job.

Getting Access

Now, how do you get access to your own record?

You have to get in touch with a local credit bureau that has your report on file, then request a copy of your report.

If you have recently been turned down for credit, you have the right to get a free copy of your report. The store or company that rejected your credit application must supply the name of the credit bureau that provided the report. Write or call that credit bureau, provide information about the credit denial, and ask for a copy of the report.

If you have not been denied credit, there are three ways to find out the name of a credit bureau in your area:

1. Look in the Yellow Pages under *credit reporting agencies*. Not all Yellow Pages have this listing, but if yours does, at least one of the companies under that heading will probably have your credit record on file.

2. Look in the White Pages for the names of the five largest credit bureaus in the country. They are:

- Equifax (based in Atlanta)
- TRW Information Systems Co. (Cleveland)

- Trans-Union Credit Information Co. (Chicago)
- Chilton (Dallas)
- Pinger (Houston)

These companies have many local offices. If there's one in your area, it will be listed in the phone book.

3. Ask a bank officer to identify a credit bureau that is used by local businesses.

Call the credit bureau, ask for the consumer relations department, and tell the representative that you are requesting a copy of your credit record. The representative will tell you where to address your written request and what information to include in your request. Most credit bureaus will ask you to provide your name, address, social security number, and date of birth. In addition, some bureaus may request one or two credit card numbers.

If you have been denied credit within the past 30 days, send in a copy of the letter of denial along with the request

■ **IS YOUR REPORT ACCURATE?**

According to industry statistics about nine million requests for information from credit bureaus are made every year. About one half of 1 percent are inaccurate. (But this is the industry talking, so the actual number could be considerably higher.) The credit bureau relies largely on information that is given to it by various creditors or businesses. The bureau does little real investigation on its own. Among the reasons for inaccuracies:

- The record might list the bad debts of another person with a similar name.
- It might include tax liens or judgments that have been satisfied.
- It might include disputes with merchants that have been resolved.
- It might have out-of-date employer information.

for your credit record so you will not be charged for requesting a report. If you have not been denied credit, there's a service charge usually ranging from about $8 to $20. For an additional charge you can also request your spouse's credit record.

What the Credit Bureaus Report

According to the Fair Credit Reporting Act of 1971, you have a legal right to know everything that's in your file, and you also have a right to take steps to correct information that's inaccurate. If you've never checked it before, you may wonder how you look in that little financial profile. Do you have a "good" credit rating or a "bad" credit rating? Is there a big blot next to your name or a star for good behavior?

The credit bureau doesn't make a judgment either way. That is, the bureau doesn't tell creditors, businesses, or potential employers whether you're a good or bad credit risk or a good or bad employment risk. The bureau simply repeats the data that have been provided to it by others. Amid that data:

- Your name, social security number, current employer, former employer, recent and current addresses, and possibly your income
- Similar information about your spouse
- How many lines of credit you have with how many lending institutions
- A history of payment patterns for the last two years: whether you paid a bill within 30, 60, 90, 120, or over 120 days and whether you are making regular payments under a wage-earner plan (see "Tactic 8: Bankruptcy")
- A record of any foreclosures, bankruptcies, or liens against you; any repossession or voluntary reposses-

sion; bad debt, charged-off account, or collection accounts
- A record of accounts that have been closed out
- A record of the other lending institutions that have made inquiries within the past six months

All this information has been reported to the credit bureau by banks, finance companies, merchants, credit card companies, and other creditors. As a matter of course, whenever a loan or line of credit is issued to you, the amount and terms are sent in to the credit bureau. In addition, some information is collected by the credit bureaus from other sources, such as court records.

Most information is kept in your open file for seven years. Anyone wanting to see your file must furnish some evidence that your record is being requested for approved purposes. It may be sent to someone who will use it in connection with a credit transaction, employment, underwriting of insurance, determination of eligibility for a license, or any other business transaction. Anyone obtaining a credit report for personal reasons—or anyone misrepresenting their business—may be subjected to legal action.

"GOOD" RISK OR "BAD" RISK?

Anyone who looks at your credit record can draw his or her own conclusions. The inquirer can find out whether you frequently move or change jobs. He or she can compare your income level (if it's given) to the outstanding lines of credit and can find out how quickly you pay your bills. In addition, the person inquiring can see which other companies made inquiries. (If those companies are not subsequently listed among your creditors, it indicates that they declined to give you credit.) If a store, credit card issuer, or lending institution is making the inquiry, that company will assign you a rating based on all these relevant factors.

Correcting the Record

What do you do if information in your file is inaccurate?

By law you may request verification of all the information in your record. The company that supplied that information must confirm it by responding within a "reasonable" length of time, which is considered to be 30 days. If the disputed account is not verified in 30 days, that information should be erased from your record.

After the record has been corrected, you have a right under the federal Fair Credit Reporting Act to request that the corrected report be mailed to any business that checked your credit rating during the past six months or to any potential employer who has checked within the past two years.

YOUR RIGHT TO A STATEMENT

If you aren't satisfied with the investigation of your claim, you can write a statement (up to 100 words) explaining the situation and have the statement entered in your file. The statement is not an argument; it should simply state the facts. (For instance, "I have the canceled check to Carry-On Credit, Inc., that shows I paid within 30 days.")

However, the statement does not need to dispute the record; it can provide an explanation. You can explain that your creditors have not corrected erroneous information; you can state when delinquent accounts were paid; and you can explain where illness, accident, or unemployment got you into temporary trouble. Your statement can also supply favorable information that has not been included in the record. In the future, whenever your credit record is sent out in response to an inquiry, your statements must be included.

The time frame is 30 days for the original investigation, another 30 days for a reinvestigation (if you request it), then 30 days for you to file a statement that will go in your permanent record. The credit bureau will then include your statement with any report that goes out to anyone making future inquiries.

Do You Need a Credit Clinic?

You may see ads for agencies that promise to "clean up" your credit rating, "erase black marks" against you, and obtain new credit cards on your behalf. These are "credit clinics."

A credit clinic is any service that offers to erase a "bad" credit record and open up a new line of credit for you. These clinics also go by other names ("credit repair service," for instance), and they solicit business in a variety of ways.

If you don't like the way your credit record looks, you might be tempted to contact one of these services. However, credit clinics do only what you can do yourself—request your credit record and then request verification of information in the file. The only difference is that they take a heavy-bombardment approach, demanding verification of *every* item. In addition, they may be able to help you obtain a new out-of-state credit card charging the highest rate of interest. For these services they charge fees that range from $150 to $1,000. Needless to say, anyone with a credit problem needs this additional expense about as much as a case of cholera.

If you have carefully checked your credit report, updated favorable information, challenged and corrected inaccuracies, and included statements for the record, you have done everything you can right now to "fix" your credit profile. Every month that you stay current on your payments and pay off charge cards and credit cards, you are creating a *new* profile of creditworthiness.

BANKRUPTCY

Just about the only reason you would want to declare personal bankruptcy is that you've tried every other alternative and you just can't figure out another way. If you do have to declare bankruptcy, you can anticipate some emotional consequences: it just doesn't feel good. You can also expect financial consequences: bankruptcy makes it very difficult to get new credit. Essentially, you have to start building up your creditworthiness all over again.

On the other hand, declaring bankruptcy is definitely not the end of the world. Millions of 20th-century Americans have survived personal bankruptcy quite nicely—without becoming street people, social outcasts, or indigents. Bankruptcy is not punishment for past errors and omissions. Instead it's an opportunity to clean the slate and start over again. And even though the fact of bankruptcy will remain on your credit record for 10 years, adversely affecting your ability to get credit, lending and credit companies have various policies. You may be able to get credit despite the bankruptcy if you can show income and you have no debt, or you may be able to borrow money with a cosigner or a third-party guarantee.

All bankruptcy really means is that your expenses have exceeded your income. When you declare bankruptcy, you have the opportunity to reorganize so that, in the future, your income will exceed your expenses once again. In a business sense you are making your household solvent.

Your First Move: Get a Lawyer

For a bankruptcy proceeding you definitely need the help of an attorney who is experienced in bankruptcy. You can find a bankruptcy lawyer in your area through a legal referral service in your state or county (see "Resource 3: Attorneys").

The first thing an attorney can do for you is suggest perfectly feasible alternatives to bankruptcy. He or she might intervene directly with your creditors or might recommend other ways you can become solvent again.

If indeed bankruptcy is the only solution, you'll need an attorney to decide which type of personal bankruptcy you should claim. Then you will need the representation of a lawyer before the bankruptcy court. The attorney will see that you receive the assets to which you are entitled and the full protection of the court under the bankruptcy law.

Types of Personal Bankruptcy

Under the federal code there are two kinds of personal bankruptcy, Chapter 13 and Chapter 7.

SOME TERMINOLOGY

The terminology of bankruptcy tells you a lot about what it is and what it does. So here's a mini-glossary:

Bankruptcy Court

This is a federal court that has nothing to do with any kind of criminal court or criminal proceedings. Judges of the federal court are specifically assigned to hear bankruptcy cases and to appoint trustees. The trustee appointed by the court is then responsible for handling all matters related to the assets and liabilities of the debtor. Point of clarification: The court is not, in any way, prosecuting or going after the debtor. On the contrary, the purpose of the trustee is to protect the debtor from being hounded, pursued, or harassed by creditors.

Discharge a Debt

What this means is that the debt is eliminated. When a debt has been discharged, the debtor no longer has an obligation to pay it, and the creditor has no right to claim it. In a bankruptcy proceeding most debts (such as credit card balances) can be discharged, but some, such as income taxes owed, cannot.

A Stay

The stay is the power of the bankruptcy court to impose a freeze on any actions against the person who declares bankruptcy. Anyone who attempts to violate the stay of the court may be subject to imprisonment or severe fines.

The stay forestalls all lawsuits and claims. If there's a foreclosure action against you because of failure to make your mortgage payment, the stay will stop that legal proceeding until the estate has been settled by the bankruptcy court. As long as the stay is in force, the IRS cannot levy your property to pay back taxes or put a lien on your income or bank account. The stay forces all creditors to lift existing liens on your home or property.

Preferences

If a debtor settles up with one creditor, leaving others in the lurch shortly before going bankrupt, this is considered a *preference*. For instance, if a debtor who faces bankruptcy decides to pay the last $1,000 from his bank account to cousin Ted and not a penny to MasterCard, this is obviously a preference toward cousin Ted. The bankruptcy court can "set aside" that preference. The judge will order cousin Ted to pay back the $1,000 so it can be distributed equally; or, if he can't or won't, the person who declares bankruptcy will be allowed to keep $1,000 less of his assets.

Conveyances

Another evasion the bankruptcy court is likely to block is a conveyance of property to another person shortly before bankruptcy is declared. If you see bankruptcy on the horizon and convey property to cousin Ted, the court will attempt to get that property back or to penalize you during the discharge of debts.

CHAPTER 13

If you choose Chapter 13 bankruptcy, the judge and trustee of the court will develop a wage-earner plan for the repayment of outstanding debts. You state what your income and expenses are expected to be, and the court imposes a stay preventing any other action against you. The bankruptcy trustee collects a certain amount of income from you every month and pays it out to your creditors. Being put on a wage-earner plan under Chapter 13 shows up on your credit report.

The advantage of Chapter 13 is that all interest payments on outstanding debt automatically come to a halt. The outstanding debt then assumes the form of a fixed-term loan, with no interest remaining on the balance. So, as long as your income and expenses are stable, Chapter 13 is an effective way to eliminate current debts.

The disadvantages, however, include the fact that the pay-back arrangement may be very similar to what you could negotiate *without* declaring bankruptcy, and Chapter 13 does show up on your credit report, where it will appear for the next 10 years, warning potential lenders that you are a poor credit risk. In addition, if your income and expenses are not stable, and you end up not being able to make payments to the trustee, you might have to declare Chapter 7 bankruptcy.

CHAPTER 7

You would choose Chapter 7 bankruptcy only if you and your attorney decide you have no alternative.

Under Chapter 7 the bankruptcy court discharges nearly all of your debts, except taxes, alimony and child support, fines, and certain other debts such as student loans. While these cannot be discharged under bankruptcy law, the court can issue a stay so that you do not have to make immediate payment.

You have the right to receive social security, unemployment compensation, welfare, VA disability, support, and certain pension benefits, and spouses get a double exemption for these payments and benefits. You are also allowed to keep a certain amount of property, according to either federal or state exemptions, and your attorney will help you decide which are more advantageous.

Federal exemptions allow you to keep up to $17,800 (or $35,600 for a husband and wife) worth of property:

FEDERAL EXEMPTIONS

Residential property	$7,500
Or, for a non-homeowner, the maximum exemption is:	3,750

A motor vehicle	1,200
Household furnishings or other consumer goods	200
Aggregate value	4,000
Jewelry for personal use	500
Loan or cash surrender value in a life insurance policy	4,000
Additional	400

State exemptions vary. (When former Secretary of the Treasury John Connally declared bankruptcy in Texas, under the state of Texas bankruptcy code he was allowed to keep 25 acres plus a horse and buggy. He chose the state deduction, presumably for the valuable acreage rather than for the horse and buggy.)

What Happens When You File

1. When you file for bankruptcy under Chapter 13 or Chapter 7, your counsel will prepare a petition outlining "dischargeable" and "nondischargeable" debts.

2. Then you will usually be asked to appear in court for a hearing. During the hearing you tell the bankruptcy trustee why you're in debt and why you're filing.

3. After the hearing the court will determine what debts are to be discharged and in what order.

4. After you file for bankruptcy, the bankruptcy court puts an automatic stay on your accounts and property. As of that date your creditors cannot place a levy on your property to collect money. (Any creditor who violates the automatic stay is subject to contempt-of-court proceedings.) Under the stay a landlord can be stopped from evicting you, and a bank or mortgage company can be prevented from foreclosing on your home. If there is an IRS levy on your bank account, it will be lifted by order of the bankruptcy court. Nonexempt assets will be sold and used toward payment of debts. If you have only exempt assets,

they cannot be used to pay off your debts. Creditors in a "no-asset" case can't sue the debtor after the bankruptcy is filed.

5. After a bankruptcy filing, as you acquire assets, you will be liable for those debts that could not be discharged under the bankruptcy code, including taxes, alimony, child support, and student loans. However, other creditors cannot pursue you for repayment. Your charges to them have been forever discharged.

III

RESOURCES

RESOURCE 1 ......

FAMILY AND FRIENDS

....

How much you ask for help and how much you tell
your relatives and friends about your financial situation all
depends on the relationships you have with those people.
For some of you such requests may be fraught with difficulty, and you'll probably want to steer clear. But if family
ties and friendships are strong, kith and kin may be able to
help you in numerous ways.

Family

First of all, if you've radically changed your spending
patterns, let relatives know why. In all probability they've
been through similar circumstances themselves, and they
may be very sympathetic. Your new budget might not allow

you to make long-distance trips to visit family as often as you used to. Nor will you be able to continue lavish gift giving. Best policy: Let them know why. Better that they should know you're financially strapped than that they think you don't *want* to visit or give them gifts anymore.

If you want them to know what action you're taking, describe the six-step action plan—or show them this book.

DIRECT FINANCIAL ASSISTANCE

If you need temporary financial help, can you turn to your relatives? The best way to answer this question might be to look at your "track record." Have you previously borrowed money from a relative for a car, an educational loan, or a down payment on a house? If so, did you pay back the agreed-upon amount? Was the loan handled in a businesslike way, or did it drastically interfere with family relationships?

In all probability history will be repeated. (Families tend to work that way.) If a previous financial matter caused more trouble than it was worth, the problems will likely again outweigh the worth if you ask for another loan. On the other hand, if the loan was given easily, accepted graciously, and paid back as agreed, you can probably count on help from the same relative now.

OTHER WAYS YOUR FAMILY CAN HELP

Apart from the financial side, be sure to consider other important ways that family members might be willing to give you a hand:

- Perhaps you've always been the "helper-outer" in the family—the one to entertain, to lend money to brother Billy, or to take on full care of an aging parent. If these have been solo responsibilities, you'll need to negotiate with other family members so the helping-out is shared in the future.

- If you have children who need child care so you and your spouse can work outside the home, you might ask nearby relatives if they can help.
- If you need home furnishings or household items that you can't afford right now, perhaps relatives can help provide them. Maybe they're planning to replace the living room couch or they have extra furniture or appliances stored in the basement or attic.
- Think about ways that relatives can help you with vacation plans. If you (or you and your spouse) are looking for ways to cut down on vacation costs, maybe there's a family summer cabin that's going unused. Or perhaps cousin Fred has a time-share in a Florida condominium that he hasn't visited in the past three winters. If your relatives know you're looking for an inexpensive getaway, they might have ideas, suggestions, or even a place you can use.
- If you're married with children, you may actually get some vacation time at home if grandparents or other relatives will take the children. Often it's a treat for the kids to visit the relatives, and a grandchild-loving grandparent may relish the opportunity to take on the challenge. Meanwhile, you and your spouse get a vacation at home—reexperiencing the reckless abandon of being child-free.

Turning to Friends

For a while at least, your action plan may appear to your friends like a "Just Say No to Everything" campaign. Relationships are likely to be affected. Can you confide in your friends? They may *want* the opportunity to help—and they may turn out to be wonderful resources. If in doubt, give them the chance.

Here are some ways good friends can offer support and reinforcement:

- If they know you're looking for additional work—possibly free-lance or part-time—they might have some great leads you can pursue.
- If you need help finding an attorney or getting advice on tax planning, your friends may be able to recommend qualified people.
- When you're looking for cheap places to eat, reasonable places to stay, or bargains of various kinds, ask friends.
- If it turns out that your friends are just as eager to cut back on their spending as you are (and that's very likely!), get together to plot and plan expense-saving entertainment and vacations. You may be able to figure out very cheap ways to entertain. How about taking turns hosting informal dinner parties instead of getting together at the latest trendy bistro? If you have children, you can easily swap baby-sitting services. (Maybe swap day care too, if your schedules mesh.) And if the compatibility factor is high all around, you might even share a vacation house, splitting the rent among several families.

CREDIT COUNSELING

· ·

Credit counseling is a service provided to consumers by a number of private and public agencies around the country. Unlike a "credit clinic" or "credit repair service" that promises to erase a bad credit record, credit counselors simply work with you to create a household budget plan and negotiate with your creditors.

How to Get Credit Counseling

A not-for-profit organization called the Consumer Credit Counseling Service (CCCS)—under an umbrella organization known as the National Foundation for Consumer Credit (NFCC)—has, in offices around the country, experienced counselors who help consumers work out budget plans and meet their credit obligations. The charge for such services ranges from zero to about $10 a month.

The National Foundation for Consumer Credit can charge little or nothing for its services because it is largely supported by businesses that extend credit to consumers. Contributions from business to the NFCC are voluntary, but the organization asks creditors to return a "fair share" (7 to 15 percent) of what they receive from debtors who are on the CCCS debt repayment program. In general the businesses that are the largest beneficiaries of the debt-repayment program are also the largest contributors to CCCS.

This is not by any means secret information. But naturally it creates a bias. The CCCS office is interested in seeing that you work out a budget or get on a repayment plan that will allow you to settle up with your creditors. Of course you have the benefit of free or almost-free counseling, as well as the help of a counselor who will actually handle the debt repayment negotiations with your creditors.

If the only questions are how you'll repay your creditors and on what terms, CCCS may be a most desirable resource for you. The national organization has been going since 1951, and it is well established around the country. As of the end of 1989 there were 479 offices.

The budget and credit counseling services offered are available with no obligation, and it will be entirely your choice whether you sign up for the debt repayment program. An initial visit can tell you whether the CCCS office has the resources that will be helpful to you. Then you can decide whether to use these resources, set up your own program, or look elsewhere. (If you want additional information on the National Foundation for Consumer Credit, you can contact NFCC, 8701 Georgia Avenue, Suite 507, Silver Spring, MD 20910; 301-589-5600.)

To quickly get in touch with the Consumer Credit Counseling Service in your area, call 800-388-CCCS from a Touch-Tone phone. A recorded voice will ask you to enter your area code, then another recorded voice will provide information about nearby CCCS offices. If there's an office close by, call and set up an appointment or find out when you can visit.

You will speed up the whole process by taking along data about income, expenses, savings, the amounts you owe to creditors, and relevant account numbers. It's a good idea to take along any member of your household who's involved in your home budget or liable for some of your debts—your spouse, partner, and grown children if they are living with you and incurring or sharing expenses.

When you arrive, the counselor will sit down with you and review income, expenses, and outstanding debt. If it looks as if you need an attorney, the counselor will refer you elsewhere, since CCCS doesn't do any legal work. (According to CCCS, about 30 percent of those who visit their offices are referred to legal aid or to a legal referral service.) If the counselor decides that you need personal, family, or marital counseling, you will be referred to services outside CCCS. But if it's strictly a matter of wrestling with your budget, coming up with a repayment plan, and/ or dealing with creditors, the counselor at CCCS will work closely with you.

What a Counselor Does

There are basically three categories of help that this service provides:

BUDGET COUNSELING

The counselor reviews your budget in detail and queries you about areas where you may be underestimating or overspending. He or she may then suggest some alternative budget plans that would allow you to save more and spend less. The counselor may also suggest ways that you can increase your household income.

CREDIT COUNSELING

If you're not using credit to your best advantage, the counselor may be able to suggest sources of loans at reduced interest rates or may advise you about consolidating your loans. You can also obtain general information about using credit. Credit counseling, like budget counseling, is always free of charge.

DEBT REPAYMENT

About 40 percent of those who visit the CCCS offices choose to go on a debt repayment plan. After discussing your budget with you, the counselor from CCCS will negotiate with your creditors to find out whether they will accept your proposed repayment plan.

Because CCCS maintains good relations with creditors and has prior experience in dealing with them, the CCCS counselors know what kind of repayment plan is likely to be accepted by credit card companies, nationwide department stores, and other businesses. They also know which businesses are likely to forgive the interest if the debtor agrees to repayment of the full principal. If you work with CCCS, you can be assured that arrangements with creditors will, in all likelihood, be handled efficiently. Be aware, however, that CCCS is interested in seeing that creditors eventually get full payment on their accounts.

Probably the best way to use the CCCS debt repayment plan is when you have already decided that you want to work out a fair pay-back arrangement but want to avoid the hassle of negotiating separately with each creditor.

Once the debt repayment plan is accepted by creditors, you agree not to incur any further debt. (Some families choose to relinquish their credit cards to their CCCS counselor for the duration of the program.) Each month you turn over a portion of your income to the CCCS office; then CCCS settles with each of your creditors out of your partial income payments. As long as your income and your payments to CCCS remain steady, everything will be paid off and you'll receive no more notices from your creditors.

The full repayment period varies, depending on the extent of your indebtedness, but rarely extends beyond five years. In many cases full repayment can be made within three years.

Other Credit Counseling Services

In addition to the nationwide CCCS there are a number of community-sponsored credit counseling services that usually do not charge a fee. To find out whether there is one in your area, check the listings in the "Human Resources" section of your phone book or call a general information number for your city or county.

A community-funded service probably does not negotiate with creditors in the same way CCCS does, but its credit counseling may be more objective. Budget counseling may be similar at both services. Incidentally, if it's budget or credit counseling you want, there's nothing to stop you from visiting both a CCCS office and community-sponsored service and comparing the advice you get at both places.

ATTORNEYS

■ ■

It won't be news to anyone that legal counsel is usually expensive. If you can negotiate with creditors on your own, or if you use a resource such as the Consumer Credit Counseling Service (see "Resource 2") to handle your situation, you probably don't need an attorney. And you don't need a lawyer to handle your finances.

On the other hand, we have already mentioned a number of situations where a lawyer is not only helpful but necessary. If you are seriously considering personal bankruptcy, then by all means talk to a lawyer about the alternatives and the consequences. And if you are being harassed by creditors or by collection agencies, a lawyer may help defend you from unlawful actions or proceedings. You also urgently need a lawyer if the holder of your mortgage is threatening to foreclose on your house.

You should be aware that most attorneys would prefer to handle negotiations on your behalf from the very beginning. They want to make sure that by negotiating on your own, you don't forfeit a defense. If you hire an attorney after you have already started to negotiate with a creditor or tax authority, be sure to fully inform your counsel of all the conversations and correspondence that have occurred to date.

What If There's Direct Legal Action?

Other situations that probably require a lawyer are direct legal actions against you. If a summons to appear in court has been delivered by a creditor, you may have 20 or 30 days to respond. *Don't ignore a summons!* The best procedure is to have your own lawyer call the creditor's lawyers and discuss whatever arrangements you can make for repayment of the loan. In some circumstances the creditor's lawyers will cancel the summons—but if the case does go to court, you will probably be more successful with legal counsel.

If the creditor garnishees your wages, repossesses your property, or issues a deficiency judgment, you need an attorney on your side. Garnishment occurs when the creditor obtains the legal right to take repayment directly from your wages, and your employer is required to comply. In the case of repossession, the creditor can seize property that you have used for security and sell the goods to repay the balance of your loan. If, after such a sale, there is still a balance owed, the creditor can return to the court for a deficiency judgment. This would allow the creditor to seize other possessions and sell them to pay off the balance.

If any of these situations arises, you may still be able to settle with the creditor by working out a repayment plan. However, if you can't come up with a repayment plan immediately, there may be legal remedies to prevent further legal action. You'll probably be more successful in protecting your rights and property if you have an attorney.

In any of the situations discussed in Part II—landlord disputes, foreclosure, and bankruptcy—you need an attorney who is experienced in that specific area of the law.

How to Find a Lawyer

The American Bar Association authorizes "Lawyers' Reference Services" and "Lawyers' Referral Services" throughout the country. These services are listed under "Human Services" in many telephone books.

If you can't find the listing in the book, you can call the American Bar Association (located in Chicago), ask for Information Services, and then request the telephone number of the legal referral service nearest you. Outside Illinois the number to call to reach the ABA is 800-621-6159. If you are calling from Illinois, the number is 312-988-5000.

When you call your local referral service, a representative will ask what kind of legal help you need. The service will give you the name and telephone number of an attorney in your county. The referral is usually confirmed by mail.

Along with the confirmation, you may receive a printed agreement that entitles you to an initial consultation with the recommended attorney for a minimal fee—for example, a half-hour consultation for $20. Any arrangements you make with the lawyer after the first consultation are up to you. (The referral service does not set fees.)

If you are unable to pay anything for a lawyer, call legal aid, usually found among city government or "Human Services" listings in the telephone book. To qualify for legal aid you have to undergo an initial screening. If you prove the need for an attorney and your income is sufficiently small, you will be referred to a lawyer who will provide further counsel free of charge.

DEBTORS ANONYMOUS

Debtors Anonymous is an organization that's structured almost exactly like Alcoholics Anonymous, but it's for chronic debtors rather than chronic drinkers. One of the interesting things about this organization is that many people get deeply into debt by overspending for many of the same reasons that people become alcoholics by drinking. Like drugs and alcohol, spending provides instant escape (and later regrets). It's a way to "cure" low self-esteem. It even affects those around us in similar ways; chronic debt, like alcoholism, is associated with many kinds of family stress.

It therefore makes perfect sense to structure an organization like Debtors Anonymous on the same foundation as Alcoholics Anonymous. As the title implies, anonymity is maintained. Meetings are held in the evenings, generally in churches and public buildings. Those who attend introduce themselves by their first names only. As the preamble of Debtors Anonymous states, "The only requirement for membership is a desire to stop using any form of unsecured debt."

Debtors Anonymous can be very effective for a number of reasons. First, you have the gratification of being in an organization where all the members admit they're in the same boat. They talk openly about their struggles, and they're very honest about what got them into trouble in the first place and what they're doing to recover.

For information, write to Debtors Anonymous, General Service Board, P.O. Box 20322, New York, NY 10025-9992.

IV

APPENDIXES

APPENDIX A:
WORKSHEETS FOR
ACTION STEP 1

EXPENSE WORKSHEET

EXPENSE	WEEK 1	WEEK 2	WEEK 3	WEEK 4	TOTAL	GOAL
GENERAL WEEKLY EXPENSES						
Food/beverages: grocery store items only	☐	☐	☐	☐	☐	$_____
Food/beverages: take-out for home	☐	☐	☐	☐	☐	$_____
Food/beverages: office snacks, lunches	☐	☐	☐	☐	☐	$_____
Beer/wine/other alcoholic beverages	☐	☐	☐	☐	☐	$_____
Cigarettes/tobacco	☐	☐	☐	☐	☐	$_____
Clothing purchases (for adults)	☐	☐	☐	☐	☐	$_____
Laundry/cleaning items for home	☐	☐	☐	☐	☐	$_____
Laundry/dry-cleaning costs outside home	☐	☐	☐	☐	☐	$_____
Nonprescription drugs/medicine	☐	☐	☐	☐	☐	$_____
Cosmetic items	☐	☐	☐	☐	☐	$_____
Periodicals	☐	☐	☐	☐	☐	$_____
Pet supplies	☐	☐	☐	☐	☐	$_____
Hobby supplies	☐	☐	☐	☐	☐	$_____
Other general weekly expenses						
_____	☐	☐	☐	☐	☐	$_____
_____	☐	☐	☐	☐	☐	$_____

HOUSEHOLD SERVICES

Cleaning	☐	☐	☐	☐	☐	$_____
Doorman/building services	☐	☐	☐	☐	☐	$_____
Trash removal	☐	☐	☐	☐	☐	$_____
Repairs by professionals (plumber, electrician, etc.)	☐	☐	☐	☐	☐	$_____
Lawn care/snow removal	☐	☐	☐	☐	☐	$_____
Maid	☐	☐	☐	☐	☐	$_____
Gardener	☐	☐	☐	☐	☐	$_____

Other household services:

_____	☐	☐	☐	☐	☐	$_____
_____	☐	☐	☐	☐	☐	$_____

HOUSE/GARDEN ITEMS

Landscaping items	☐	☐	☐	☐	☐	$_____
Furnishings	☐	☐	☐	☐	☐	$_____
Painting/wallpapering/ decorating	☐	☐	☐	☐	☐	$_____
Appliances	☐	☐	☐	☐	☐	$_____
Tools/equipment	☐	☐	☐	☐	☐	$_____

Other house/garden items:

_____	☐	☐	☐	☐	☐	$_____
_____	☐	☐	☐	☐	☐	$_____

TRANSPORTATION

Car: Gas/oil ☐ ☐ ☐ ☐ ☐ $_____

Car: Tolls ☐ ☐ ☐ ☐ ☐ $_____

Car: Parking ☐ ☐ ☐ ☐ ☐ $_____

Car: Repairs/maintenance ☐ ☐ ☐ ☐ ☐ $_____

Train/bus/subway fare ☐ ☐ ☐ ☐ ☐ $_____

Taxi/limo ☐ ☐ ☐ ☐ ☐ $_____

Other transportation
expenses:

_____ ☐ ☐ ☐ ☐ ☐ $_____

_____ ☐ ☐ ☐ ☐ ☐ $_____

**ENTERTAINMENT AND
RECREATION**

Entertainment: shows,
films, events ☐ ☐ ☐ ☐ ☐ $_____

Entertainment: dining/
drinking ☐ ☐ ☐ ☐ ☐ $_____

Entertainment: books,
tapes, records, CDs,
videos, software ☐ ☐ ☐ ☐ ☐ $_____

Recreation: sports/health ☐ ☐ ☐ ☐ ☐ $_____

Other entertainment/
recreation expenses:

_____ ☐ ☐ ☐ ☐ ☐ $_____

_____ ☐ ☐ ☐ ☐ ☐ $_____

GIFTS ☐ ☐ ☐ ☐ ☐ $_____

HOME-OFFICE SUPPLIES

Desk items ☐ ☐ ☐ ☐ ☐ $_____

Cards and stationery ☐ ☐ ☐ ☐ ☐ $_____

Postage and mailing ☐ ☐ ☐ ☐ ☐ $_____

Other home-office supplies:

_____ ☐ ☐ ☐ ☐ ☐ $_____

_____ ☐ ☐ ☐ ☐ ☐ $_____

MEDICAL EXPENSES
(Not covered
by insurance)

Medical ☐ ☐ ☐ ☐ ☐ $_____

Dental ☐ ☐ ☐ ☐ ☐ $_____

Prescriptions ☐ ☐ ☐ ☐ ☐ $_____

Treatments ☐ ☐ ☐ ☐ ☐ $_____

CHILDREN'S
EXPENSES

Allowances ☐ ☐ ☐ ☐ ☐ $_____

Baby-sitting ☐ ☐ ☐ ☐ ☐ $_____

Child care ☐ ☐ ☐ ☐ ☐ $_____

Nanny ☐ ☐ ☐ ☐ ☐ $_____

Gifts (from the children) ☐ ☐ ☐ ☐ ☐ $_____

Toys ☐ ☐ ☐ ☐ ☐ $_____

Clothing ☐ ☐ ☐ ☐ ☐ $_____

Entertainment/recreation ☐ ☐ ☐ ☐ ☐ $_____

Sports-related   □ □ □ □ □ $_____

Camp   □ □ □ □ □ $_____

Bus/train fare   □ □ □ □ □ $_____

Other children's expenses:

_____ □ □ □ □ □ $_____

_____ □ □ □ □ □ $_____

(NOTE: If any of the expenses listed below are quarterly, annual, or semiannual, calculate them on a monthly basis. For many of the expenses below, the TOTAL and the GOAL are the same. If so, enter the same amount in both the "TOTAL" and "GOAL" columns.)

EDUCATION

Tuition (self or spouse) $_____ $_____

Tuition (children) $_____ $_____

Tutoring fees $_____ $_____

School books and school
   supplies $_____ $_____

Room and board $_____ $_____

Other education expenses: $_____ $_____

_____ $_____ $_____

_____ $_____ $_____

RENT OR MORTGAGE
PAYMENT(S) $_____ $_____

PROPERTY/REAL ESTATE
   TAXES (If not included in
   mortgage payments) $_____ $_____

CAR PAYMENTS $_____ $_____

UTILITIES

Water $_____ $_____

Heat $_____ $_____

Electricity $_____ $_____

Telephone $_____ $_____

Sewer rent $_____ $_____

TV - Cable/satellite fees $_____ $_____

INSURANCE

Medical $_____ $_____

Disability $_____ $_____

Automobile $_____ $_____

Homeowners $_____ $_____

Life $_____ $_____

CLUB DUES

_____ $_____ $_____

_____ $_____ $_____

DUES TO OTHER ORGANIZATIONS

_____ $_____ $_____

_____ $_____ $_____

PAYMENTS ON EDUCATION
   LOANS $_____ $_____

PAYMENTS ON PERSONAL
  LOANS (friends, relatives) $_____ $_____

SUPPORT/ALIMONY
PAYMENTS $_____ $_____

CONTRIBUTIONS

Charitable $_____ $_____

Religious $_____ $_____

Causes $_____ $_____

Other contributions: $_____ $_____

_____ $_____ $_____

_____ $_____ $_____

TOTAL MONTHLY
EXPENSES $_____

TOTAL MONTHLY
EXPENSES—*YOUR NEW*
  GOAL $_____

CREDIT CARD AND CHARGE CARD WORKSHEET

CREDIT CARD OR CHARGE CARD	BALANCE	FINANCE CHARGE	MINIMUM PAYMENT
_____	_____	_____	_____
_____	_____	_____	_____
_____	_____	_____	_____
_____	_____	_____	_____
_____	_____	_____	_____
_____	_____	_____	_____
_____	_____	_____	_____
_____	_____	_____	_____
_____	_____	_____	_____
_____	_____	_____	_____
_____	_____	_____	_____
_____	_____	_____	_____
_____	_____	_____	_____
_____	_____	_____	_____
_____	_____	_____	_____
_____	_____	_____	_____
_____	_____	_____	_____

TOTAL BALANCE _____

TOTAL FINANCE CHARGES _____

TOTAL MINIMUM CREDIT CARD/CHARGE CARD PAYMENTS _____

INCOME WORKSHEET

EARNED INCOME	MONTHLY
Earner #1: Salary / wages after taxes	_____
Earner #2: Salary / wages after taxes	_____
Other Earners: Salary / wages after taxes	_____

AFTER-TAX INCOME FROM OTHER SOURCES
   (Specify—and calculate on a monthly basis.)

_____   _____

_____   _____

_____   _____

_____   _____

ADD TO GET . . .

TOTAL MONTHLY TAKE-HOME INCOME   _____ (A)

TO COMPARE YOUR INCOME WITH YOUR MONTHLY
EXPENSES . . .

   ENTER TOTAL MONTHLY EXPENSES . . .
   (from your Expense Worksheet)   _____

   ENTER TOTAL MINIMUM CREDIT CARD/CHARGE CARD PAY-
   MENTS
   (from your Credit Card and Charge Card Worksheet)   _____

ADD TO GET . . .

TOTAL MONTHLY PAYMENTS AND EXPENSES   _____ (B)

TO FIND OUT YOUR TOTAL EXCESS OR SHORTFALL AT THE END OF
THE MONTH, SUBTRACT B FROM A:

(THIS IS YOUR ONE-MONTH FINANCIAL PROFILE)   _____

APPENDIX B:
WORKSHEET FOR
ACTION STEP 3

EXPENSE	CASH EXPENSE? (YES/NO)		MONTHLY GOAL FOR THIS ITEM
GENERAL WEEKLY EXPENSES			
Food/beverages: grocery store items only	YES	NO	$_____
Food/beverages: take-out for home	YES	NO	$_____
Food/beverages: office snacks, lunches	YES	NO	$_____
Beer/wine/other alcoholic beverages	YES	NO	$_____
Cigarettes/tobacco	YES	NO	$_____
Clothing purchases (for adults)	YES	NO	$_____
Laundry/cleaning items for home	YES	NO	$_____
Laundry/dry-cleaning costs outside home	YES	NO	$_____
Nonprescription drugs/medicine	YES	NO	$_____
Cosmetic items	YES	NO	$_____
Periodicals	YES	NO	$_____
Pet supplies	YES	NO	$_____
Hobby supplies	YES	NO	$_____
Other general weekly expenses:			
_____	YES	NO	$_____
_____	YES	NO	$_____
HOUSEHOLD SERVICES			
Cleaning	YES	NO	$_____
Doorman/building services	YES	NO	$_____
Trash removal	YES	NO	$_____
Repairs by professionals (plumber, electrician, etc.)	YES	NO	$_____
Lawn care/snow removal	YES	NO	$_____
Maid	YES	NO	$_____

Gardener	YES	NO	$_____

Other household services:

_____	YES	NO	$_____
_____	YES	NO	$_____

HOUSE/GARDEN ITEMS

Landscaping items	YES	NO	$_____
Furnishings	YES	NO	$_____
Painting/wallpapering/decorating	YES	NO	$_____
Appliances	YES	NO	$_____
Tools/equipment	YES	NO	$_____

Other house/garden items:

_____	YES	NO	$_____
_____	YES	NO	$_____

TRANSPORTATION

Car: Gas/oil	YES	NO	$_____
Car: Tolls	YES	NO	$_____
Car: Parking	YES	NO	$_____
Car: Repairs/maintenance	YES	NO	$_____
Train/bus/subway fare	YES	NO	$_____
Taxi/limo	YES	NO	$_____

Other transportation expenses:

_____	YES	NO	$_____
_____	YES	NO	$_____

ENTERTAINMENT AND RECREATION

Entertainment: shows, films, events	YES	NO	$_____
Entertainment: dining/drinking	YES	NO	$_____
Entertainment: books, tapes, records, CDs, videos, software	YES	NO	$_____
Recreation: sports/health	YES	NO	$_____

Other entertainment/recreation expenses:

_____	YES	NO	$_____
_____	YES	NO	$_____

GIFTS	YES	NO	$_____

HOME-OFFICE SUPPLIES

Desk items	YES	NO	$_____
Cards and stationery	YES	NO	$_____
Postage and mailing	YES	NO	$_____

Other home-office supplies:

_____	YES	NO	$_____
_____	YES	NO	$_____

MEDICAL EXPENSES
(Not covered by insurance)

Medical	YES	NO	$_____
Dental	YES	NO	$_____
Prescriptions	YES	NO	$_____
Treatments	YES	NO	$_____

CHILDREN'S EXPENSES

Allowances	YES	NO	$_____
Baby-sitting	YES	NO	$_____
Child care	YES	NO	$_____
Nanny	YES	NO	$_____
Gifts (from the children)	YES	NO	$_____
Toys	YES	NO	$_____
Clothing	YES	NO	$_____
Entertainment/recreation	YES	NO	$_____
Sports-related	YES	NO	$_____
Camp	YES	NO	$_____
Bus/train fare	YES	NO	$_____

Other children's expenses:

_____	YES	NO	$_____
_____	YES	NO	$_____

*TOTAL CASH YOU NEED ON HAND TO MEET YOUR
SPENDING GOALS DURING THE NEXT FOUR WEEKS* $_____

DIVIDE THIS TOTAL BY *FOUR* TO DETERMINE HOW MUCH
CASH YOU NEED *EACH WEEK* TO MEET YOUR SPENDING
GOALS $_____

This is your Lump-Sum, Tinker-Proof, Get-Through-the Week, Don't-Fool-Yourself
Budget Figure!

APPENDIX C:
WORKSHEET FOR
ACTION STEP 4

To complete this worksheet, you will need to refer to the three worksheets you completed previously in your Financial Profile (Appendix A).

The purpose of this worksheet is to find out how much you will be able to pay every month on your credit card and charge card accounts.

To find that amount:

First enter your TOTAL MONTHLY
TAKE-HOME INCOME from the "Income Worksheet" in Appendix A.
TOTAL MONTHLY INCOME .... $ _____ (A)

Next, enter the TOTAL MONTHLY EX-
PENSES—YOUR NEW GOAL from the
"Expense Worksheet"
in Appendix A.
TOTAL MONTHLY EXPENSES—
YOUR NEW GOAL .... $ _____ (B)

Now subtract (B) from (A) to find out
WHAT YOU CAN PAY TO YOUR
CREDITORS EVERY MONTH ...... $ _____ (C)

Now you need to compare line C with the amount you *owe* your creditors every month.

Enter the TOTAL MINIMUM CREDIT
CARD/CHARGE CARD PAYMENTS
from your "Credit Card and Charge
Card Worksheet" in Appendix A.
**TOTAL MINIMUM CREDIT CARD/
CHARGE CARD PAYMENTS** .... $ _____ (D)

Subtract line D from line C to get excess or shortage .... $ _____ (E)

APPENDIX D:
DEMYSTIFYING THE JARGON

Let's make it easy on ourselves—the world of finance has come up with some standard terms for basic money concepts. Better to remind ourselves of their definitions than to come up with a whole new lexicon.

Secured vs. Unsecured Loans

There's a fundamental difference between a loan that's secured by collateral (also referred to as a *collateral loan*) and a loan that doesn't have any security to back it up.

A **secured loan** is backed up by some kind of property. A car loan is a secured loan, with the car as the **collateral** or **security.** If you buy a car and you **default** (can't keep up with your car payments), the lender has the right to **repossess** (take back) your car, sell it at the best price, and use the income from the sale to pay off what you owe on your loan.

Similarly with a home. If it turns out that you can't meet your mortgage payments, the mortgage holder (a bank or finance company) can bring a foreclosure action. After foreclosing on the house, the mortgage holder would resell it and use profits from the sale to pay off the mortgage. That's somewhat of a simplification (see "Tactic 5:

What to Do If You Can't Meet Your Mortgage Payments" for a fuller story), but the idea is this: the actual property is the collateral on your loan.

Also in the realm of collateral loans is the **debit card loan** that is backed by investments. If you hold a debit card that's issued by a financial company or an investment firm, your stocks, bonds, or funds are security against the loan. You can use the card to make purchases or take out cash advances, but if you can't meet your payments on the card, the shortfall will be withdrawn from your investments.

Installment payments on purchases such as appliances are another kind of secured loan. If you buy a computer or washing machine "on time," you agree to make monthly payments. If you can't meet your payments for some reason, the retailer can repossess your computer or washing machine. (Since the advent of easy plastic, however, these kinds of time payments are much less prevalent than they were in Grandpa's day.)

In the Credit Card Realm

Now, what's an **unsecured loan**? Essentially it's any loan that is *not* backed by collateral. The only reason the lender believes that a borrower will pay back the unsecured loan is that the debtor has a record of doing so in the past. That's why a credit record is so important when you're looking for a loan that is not backed by some kind of collateral. (For more about your credit record, see "Tactic 7: Checking Your Credit Report.")

The money you borrow on a **credit card** is unsecured. Whether you make a purchase or get a cash advance using that card, the amount you borrow has no collateral. You are simply borrowing money from the lending institution at a high rate of interest with the promise to make installment payments at specified times. If you don't pay, the lender can't repossess your car, your stereo, or your favorite heirloom. Your account might be turned over to a collection agency, and after numerous warnings (described more fully in "Tactic 1: Dealing with Collection Agencies"), the collection agency might start talking about legal action. But the credit card issuer has no automatic right to take away any of your possessions.

A **charge account card** issued by an oil company or a department store is also an opportunity to borrow money without backing it up with your own collateral. The department store that issues a charge card give you an incentive to buy at that store, with the understanding that you'll pay back the money in installments, with interest, over time. If you pay only the minimum balance on your Frippery Charge Card or Very Refined Oil Company card, that's fine with Frippery and Very Refined. Those companies are earning terrific interest, and they have faith that you'll continue to pay your bills just because . . . well, because, statistically, nearly all of their card-holding customers do. But again, if you don't meet payments for some reason, Frippery and Very Refined can't come into your home and take your recently purchased 47 pairs of new shoes from your closet. They can do only what the credit card companies do: demand payment, turn your account over to a collection agency, and ultimately bring legal action of various kinds.

Another type of unsecured loan is a **line of credit** at the bank. If you have a line-of-credit agreement or an "automatic loan" arrangement at the bank, the bank will charge interest on the amount you're overdrawn. But the bank won't come for your 47 new pairs of shoes—even if that's where the money went.

In general, unsecured loans carry higher interest charges than collateral loans. That's because the lending institution is taking more risk. There's always the chance that a borrower might default on the loan (a certain percentage do), and the lending institution gives itself a generous allowance for sticking its neck out.

As for *who* takes the risk, it's the issuer of the card.

The issuer of a credit card might be a bank, such as Citibank, Chase, or Bank of America. Or it might be a company that's in a related service business, such as American Express or Diners Club. It might also be a somewhat more complex interstate or international lending institution that issues millions of credit cards to millions of consumers. (Banks, companies, and investment houses, incidentally, actually *sell* credit card debt in the form of huge bonds that are bought as major investments by other financial institutions. As of 1990 these bonds still had a Triple-A rating. Which means we all deserve a pat on the back. As consumers who honor our repayment commitments, the majority of us are extraordinarily reliable.)

The Revolving Credit Revolution

Undoubtedly you've heard the term **revolving line of credit.** What does it mean?

It's not quite a *Wheel of Fortune,* but close.

When you have a revolving line of credit, you don't have to pay off the full amount before you borrow more. Essentially you have only two limits on your borrowing:

1. You have to meet the monthly **minimum payment** specified by the lending institution. (This figure is, of course, printed on your monthly bill.)
2. You can't exceed the upper limit of your credit. (This is specified in the original agreement, and it's usually printed on every monthly bill you get.)

Most unsecured loans are made on a revolving credit basis, and that includes practically every credit card, charge card, and bank line of credit. As you probably realize all too well, you *don't* have to pay off your Visa, MasterCard, Discover, or Boundforglory account before the credit card issuer will generously allow you to borrow more. As long as you meet your monthly payments and don't exceed your line of credit, all those card issuers *want* you to haunt the malls, spend more, borrow more, go for that 48th pair of new shoes, whether you need them or not, and party till dawn at Le Cirque.

The only thing they don't want you to do is miss payments or exceed your line of credit. That's because your steady payments bring interest—lots of it. As for how they determine the upper credit limit . . . well, they know from your credit history that there's a certain limit to your resources. But as long as you stay within that limit, they're happy if the line of credit continues to revolve . . . and revolve . . . and revolve.

Most secured debt, on the other hand, does *not* have a revolving line of credit. A car loan has to be paid off—though of course you can always try for another loan on another car. A mortgage eventually has to be paid off. And certain kinds of bank loans have to be paid off before you can borrow more.

Liquidity

Overindebtedness is hard to measure by numbers alone, because it has more to do with **liquidity**—that is, how much income and cash on hand you have—than with the absolute amount of debt. Someone who has a payment of $20,000 due at the end of the month is not overextended if he or she can make that payment on time—*and also* meet current expenses. So, liquidity is simply the ability to come up with the cash you need, when you need it.

APPENDIX E:
BOOKS ON
INVESTMENT AND
FINANCIAL PLANNING

Breitbard, Stanley H. and Donna S. Carpenter. *The Price Waterhouse Guide to Personal Financial Planning*. New York: Henry Holt & Company, 1988.

Klein, Robert J. and the editors of *Money* magazine. *The Money Book of Money: Your Personal Financial Planner*. Boston: Little, Brown & Company, 1987.

Loeb, Marshall. *Marshall Loeb's Money Guide*. Boston: Little, Brown & Company, 1989.

Lynch, Peter with John Rothchild. *One Up on Wall Street: How to Use What You Already Know to Make Money on the Market*. New York: Penguin, 1990.

Madigan, Bob and Lawrence Kasoff. *The First-Time Investor*. Revised edition. Englewood Cliffs, New Jersey: Prentice-Hall, 1990.

Tobias, Andrew. *The Only Other Investment Guide You'll Ever Need*. New York: Bantam Books, 1989.

NOTES

HOME BUDGET SCRATCHPAD